Raising

Prophetic Kids...

Who Escort Heaven
to Earth

Jeri Williams

Raising Prophetic Kids …
Who Escort Heaven to Earth
ISBN 978-1-61584-372-5
Copyright 2009 by Jeri Williams
Mashach Publishing
1001 Avenida Pico, Suite C #331
San Clemente, CA 92673
949-813-3124
www.gracegrace.com
jeri@gracegrace.com

Printed by Advantage Graphics (949) 475-9608

CONTENTS

CHAPTER ONE

———— ∞ ————

SHECHINAH-FLAME OF MANIFESTED GLORY

Fire Bride

———— ∞ ————

It was July in sunny California and the most spectacularly beautiful day as I basked before My Lord on the front porch. The leafy fronds of a nearby palm tree, swished above my head as they rustled in the wind.

The Lord spoke as only He can. "You're like My Deborah who sat under the palm tree soaking in the prophetic anointing."

What was He meaning by this? As I sensed He was speaking of something more than, a "thus says the Lord" prophetic word. **It was as if He was nudging me to disclose the hidden Man of Jesus in** my person...in my personal presence. Like lightning, His Word shot through my soul.

> "...the testimony of Jesus
> is the spirit of prophecy."
> *REVELATION 19:10*

I was riveted to His every Word..."the spirit of prophecy is the testimony of Jesus." There it was, so clear, the true prophetic anointing gives incontrovertible evidence of Jesus. Amazing... as this season of my life I was quite the loner. In fact, I was in a season of quiet retreat as the Lord had called me to Himself as I sheltered under His arms. But yet, He still kept speaking to me of this distinguished fame He wants to unveil in His saints. My daughter:

"I'm calling this end-time generation My Heavenly Chariots... carriers of My Presence to return the glory lost in Eden. As fiery flames burning with the tangible, sensory evidence of My glory... they will testify of Me. They will be my witness' as before jurors that give evidence of My majestic splendor as it exudes from their very being. They will announce My final verdict of bringing many sons to glory. They will be My kids, clothed in My tangible presence... extraterrestrial Kids who publicize the image of God on a man and transport supernatural, invisible realities into the earthly realm. **They will be My portal between heaven and earth—MY DIVINE ADVERTISEMENT!"**

He continued to speak to my heart:

"The standard realms of prophecy have been restricted with in narrow confines. The ultimate fullness of the spirit of prophecy is when you testify of Me, revealing My likeness, My exact image spoken over you at creation? Remember when I wrote of Myself in Isaiah as being disfigured and marred, hardly recognizable? That was a prophetic glimpse of a season when My Church would be disfigured and marred, hardly recognizable as My sons of glory. But, just as a groom unveils his bride, so will My sons be beautified and dignified as Our wedding approaches. **I am Your groom that lifts the veil and reveals you in all radiance and splendor. You will truly be My "Fire Bride," dazzling and clothed in brilliance."**

Here is an amazing truth! The true prophetic anointing reveals the image of the Lord Jesus Christ in and on His saints. When the true spirit of prophecy is at work in the saints, then the image of the Man Jesus is seen. Jesus laid aside His divinity to demonstrate what a mere man fully controlled by Holy Spirit could look like and do. The true prophetic anointing reveals the image of the Lord Jesus Christ on His saints! **When the spirit of prophecy is at work then the image of the Man Jesus is seen on us.**

"But we all, with open face beholding as in a
glass the glory of the Lord, are changed into the
same image from glory to glory,
even as by the Spirit of the Lord."
2 CORINTHIANS 3:18 KJ

"Nothing between us and God, our faces shining
with the brightness of his face. And so we are
transfigured much like the Messiah,
our lives gradually becoming brighter
and more beautiful as God enters our lives
and we become like him."
2 CORINTHIANS 3:18 THE MESSAGE

Have you ever seen couples that have been
together for awhile start to look, think and talk
alike? Well, it's about to hit planet earth... the
groom and His "Fire Bride," moving as one. The
life Jesus the Man lived was not so much about
Him self, but much more about His life on earth
being our blueprint... our model to reinstate the
glory lost in Eden. He came to present a prophetic
picture of what He, the First Born, would release in
His many brethren.

Chariots—Carriers of His Glory

Abraham the Patriarch, one of God's first
prophets, was literally known as **Hashem's Chariot.**
He was called this because according to *Midrash*
(classical Rabbinic commentaries on the Hebrew
scriptures compiled between 400 and 1200 B.C.);
**one who is a bearer or carrier of God's Presence is
called a "Chariot".** *Bereshish Rabbah 47* teaches that
**the three patriarchs, Abraham, Isaac and Jacob
were bearers of the Shechinah or flame that
signified the manifested glory of God.** When
Ezekiel peered into the storm cloud and saw the
gleaming wheels rimmed with eyes, he was seeing a

flash forward of God's chariots retrieving the glory lost in the garden and returning it to earth.

The ultimate intention of our eternal Father has always been to bring many sons to glory. From eternities past, in His heart beat a heavenly vision of sons and daughters, made in His likeness. **His paternal heart has always longed for sons in the image of His One Son, Jesus.**

> "For whom He did foreknow, He also did predestinate to be conformed to the image of His Son, that He might be the first born among many brethren."
> *ROMANS 8:29 KJ*

> "For the earth shall be filled with the **knowledge (da'ath)** of the glory of the Lord as the waters cover the sea."
> *HABAKKUK 2:14 KJ*

This Hebrew word, **"da'ath,"** #1847 speaks of **experiential knowledge gained through the senses.** In other words, this expansive glory will be tangible and concretely realized, not academic.

The prophet Ezekiel saw this expansive glory when he was caught up in a heavenly vision and peered into the veiled glory cloud. **Rabinic tradition teaches the storm cloud Ezekiel saw was literally the actualization of what God had spoken in Genesis, "Let us make man in our own image and likeness."**

> "Then I looked, and, behold, a whirlwind came out of the north, a great cloud and a fire infolding itself... a brightness was about it...

as the color of amber, out of the midst of the fire...
four living creatures. And this was their
appearance; they had the likeness of a man."
EZEKIEL 1:4,5 PARTIAL KJ

What Ezekiel saw in the midst of the glory cloud was the preincarnate form of Jesus, already vibrating in anticipation of becoming the Son of Man putting on flesh. Ezekiel caught a prophetic preview of something shifting in the Godhead... Jesus would become a Man. Of course, His Spirit had always been enthroned with Holy Spirit and the Father, but something new was happening that had never been before. Ezekiel saw a prophetic glimpse of a Man forming in the heavens ... he saw the Man Jesus now in bodily form seated on the throne. What a quantum leap that God would step down, lay aside His divinity and become a Man that we might become like Him.

The Jewish scholar, R. Munk in his book, *"The World of Prayer,"* (www. innerjew.com) correlates Genesis 1:27 with Ezekiel chapter one. *"Ma'aseh bereshit"*—God's spoken decrees, His workings in Genesis are manifested or realized in *"ma'aseh merkavah"*— the workings of the chariot.

The Hebrew word, **"ma'aseh"** translates, "the work which one produces or forms; the things which God has made with His hands; the work of a poet or the fruit of righteousness." *(Gesenius' Hebrew-Chaldee Lexicon)*

The Genesis account reveals the Godhead's promise to make man in Their image; whereas **Ezekiel's vision reveals the fulfillment of how**

Jesus's likeness... His Shechinah-flame of manifested glory will return to man.

There it was, Ezekiel's privileged, open vision cracking the sky with myriads of winged cherubim returning the glory lost in the garden. Yes, God does nothing unless He first shows it to His prophets.

"God said, Let us [Father, Son and Holy Spirit] make mankind in Our image, after Our likeness, and let them have complete authority... "
GENESIS 1:26 AMPLIFIED

Cherubim Chariot

I became driven to penetrate this resplendent thunder storm... the glory... the "Shekinah" cloud. Its magnificence captured me, yet the foreboding storm clouds held an eeriness that cringed my soul. Like Ezekiel, on the banks of the Chebar River, I must peer into this glory cloud. I must see within the raging ball of glowing fire flashing forked lightnings. I couldn't be like the Israelites who stood afar off and followed a hazy glory cloud... I had to see more. **My prophetic eyes, my "nabiy seer" eyes, must infiltrate this fiery brightness and gaze upon the burning-living creatures, the cherubim and the One like a Man. For only as my eyes pierce the Spirit realm am I licensed to speak out of what I see.**

"As I looked, behold a stormy wind came out of the north, and a great cloud with a fire,

enveloping it and flashing continually; a brightness was about it and out of the midst of it there seemed to glow amber metal, out of the midst of the fire. **And out of the midst of it came the likeness of four living creatures [or cherubim]. And this was their appearance; they had the likeness of a man."**
EZEKIEL 1:4, 5 AMPLIFIED

Weren't these cherubim revealing an image of God's glory? Could it be we are intended to bear the same fire and that same glory? Could they be heavenly beings sent as examples to emulate? Did Ezekiel envision what the prophetic end-time saints would look like? Were the cherubim a pattern, a model for us to duplicate on the earth? Didn't this happen to Moses on Mt. Sinai, when God unveiled the heavenly tabernacle and then instructed him to duplicate it with precision on earth? God, You're all about, "on earth as it is in heaven."

"... David gave to Solomon his son the plan of the temple... and the place of the [ark and its] mercy seat... for the plan of the **chariot of the cherubim** that spread their wings and covered the ark of the Lord's covenant."
1 CHRONICLES 28:11,18 AMPLIFIED

God's plan is to replace the fallen anointed cherub, Lucifer, with the saints bathed in His worship. Cherubim in the Hebrew language were known to be carriers of God's glory. They were to protect and cover God's glory until they could return it to the saints on earth. Remember when God placed cherubim with a flaming sword at the entrance to Eden's garden gate?

"So [God] drove out the man; and He placed
at the east of the Garden of Eden the cherubim
and a flaming sword which turned every way,
to keep and guard the way to the tree of life."
GENESIS 3:24 AMPLIFIED

The scripture identifies Lucifer as the original
anointed cherub that covered with overshadowing
wings. He walked upon the stones of fire before the
throne of God until iniquity was found in him.

"You (Lucifer) were in Eden, the garden of God;
ever precious stone was your covering... You were
the anointed cherub that covers with overshadowing
[wings], and I set you so. You were upon the
holy mountain of God; you walked up and down
in the midst of the stones of fire...
You were blameless in your ways from the day
you were created until iniquity
and guilt were found in you."
EZEKIEL 28:13-15 PARTIAL KJ

I believe God is restoring His saints to be
"apostolic houses" operating in princely dominion
that evacuate the strong men of wicked
principalities. **I believe Ezekiel's vision of cherubim
darting like flashes of lightning with gleaming
crystal wheels full of eyes are prototypes of apostolic
saints, facilitating the return of God's glory to
earth.**

Yes, I think we all sense the impending storm
but will we have eyes to see within ... to see what
the Spirit is fashioning in the midst of the
blustering fury? What will this latter day rain look
like? I mean, how will it impact the culture, the
nations, the harvest and our kids? Oh Lord, don't

let us emaciate and domesticate this fiery storm. For anything domesticated is tamed and controlled by man. We must let it rage in all its divine fury, empowered by the Holy Ghost. **Our Savior must see His heart's desire... His One and Only Begotten Son, "bringing many sons to glory."**

CHAPTER TWO

"ℰYES" AND "WINGS"

"Eyes"—What To Do

𝒥 believe the "eyes" and "wings" in Ezekiel chapter one can be an insightful guide for raising prophetic kids... **the "eyes" speak of, what to do and the "wings" speak of, how to get there.**

"As I looked at the living creatures, I saw a wheel on the ground beside each creature ... **they sparkled like chrysolite... their rims were high and awesome, and all four rims were full of eyes all around."**
EZEKIEL 1:15,16,18 NIV

"The (cherubim)... their entire bodies, including their backs, their hands and their wings, were completely full of eyes, as were their four wheels."
EZEKIEL 10:12 NIV

What's happening here? **Eyes… eyes…**
glimmering like diamonds in the sun … immense
rims studded with prophetic eyes fastened on where
the Spirit goes and pierced with the heart of God's
intentions and will. These eyes speak of
discernment… nothing done of blind impulse but
only by the leading of Holy Spirit. These cherubim
track Holy Spirit's mood and inclinations;
traversing heaven and earth in celestial navigation…
patrolling the skyways with His divine purposes.

We can have these prophetic eyes of
discernment on how to raise kids that escort heaven
to earth. We too can patrol the celestial skyways,
scanning for divine wisdom and revelation. I
believe as we keep an open heart to the truths in the
following chapters, a personal grid, a divine
template will emerge that perfectly custom fits our
hunger for raising prophetic kids.

"Wings"– How to Get There

The wings speak of how to get there—get into
His glorious presence—riding in His cherubim
chariot where we transport heaven to earth.

> "Jehu, 'give me your hand.' So he did, and Jehu
> helped him up into the chariot. Jehu said,
> **'come with me and see my zeal for the Lord.'**
> **Then he had him ride along in his chariot.'"**
> *2 KINGS 10:15,16 NIV*

This a prophetic picture of our invitation to ride
the skyways in the cherubim chariot.

"These were the **living creatures** I had seen...
and I realized that they **were cherubim.**
Each had four faces and four wings,
and under their wings
was what looked like the hands of a man ..."
EZEKIEL 10:20, 21 NIV

The hands under the wings speak of the synergy and flow between the supernatural and the natural realm. The wings speak of being totally yielded to the workings of the Almighty God. When He moves... these cherubim move. Wings speak of the Lord's secret promptings and their being propelled not of their own power but by divine guidance. These cherubim do nothing at random but only by the prompting of the Lord's voice heard between their wings.

"**There I will meet with you** and from above the
mercy seat, from **between the two cherubim**
that are upon the ark of the Testimony.
I will speak intimately with you..."
EXODUS 25:22 AMPLIFIED

"...the cherubim lifted up their wings
to mount up from the earth..."
EZEKIEL 10:16 NIV

We see here **their wings were being carried by the wind of His Spirit... soaring and catching the blast of the Lord's breath.** They lifted their wings in worship, catching the drift of heaven. There was no flapping or tedious self-effort, just a fluttering or quivering of their wings as they ushered in the sound of God's voice.

I believe these are the same chariots that rode over the heads of the 120 gathered in the Upper Room at Pentecost. They exhaled God's sound so we could release His voice in the earth. As we wait before the Lord with our kids, we can have similar fiery paradigm shifts. Our voice will be in tandem with His and the roar of a great waterfall will swiftly execute His will.

"... suddenly there came a sound from heaven
as of a rushing mighty wind,
and it filled all the house where they were sitting."
ACTS 2:2 KJ

"Over the heads of the living creatures (cherubim) was something like a dome, shimmering like a sky full of cut glass, vaulted over their heads... When they moved I heard their wings… it was like the roar of a great waterfall, like the voice of the Strong God, like the noise of a battlefield. When they stopped, they folded their wings. And then, as they stood with folded wings, there was a voice from above the dome over their heads. Above the dome there was something that looked like a throne, sky-blue like a sapphire, with a humanlike figure towering above the throne. From what I could see, from the waist up he looked like burnished bronze and from the waist down like a blazing fire. Brightness everywhere! The way a rainbow springs out of the sky on a rainy day...

**It turned out to be the Glory of God!
When I saw all of this, I fell to my knees,
my face to the ground. Then I heard a voice."**
EZEKIEL 2:22-28 THE MESSAGE

Riding in the cherubim's chariot will cause our kids to soar heaven's skyways effortlessly... "eyes wide open" to His glory"... falling before His Magnificence in worship ... hearing the brush of angel's wings... ever so sweet... resounding His voice.

Breathy Saints

"And before the throne there was a sea of glass like unto crystal: and in the midst of the throne, and round about the throne, were four **beasts (zoons)** full of eyes before and behind."

REVELATION 4:6 KJ

This word "beast" is a Greek word **"zoons,"** #2226 derived from the word, **"Zoe,"** #2222 that translates, **"a being that has the Zoe life of God and breathes."**

Many scholars think these four "beasts" in Revelation are the same ones Ezekiel saw and called the living creatures or cherubim. They have the same four faces of lion, ox, eagle and man. The interesting point here is that **they are breathing in and out the Zoë life of God. As God exhales they inhale His divine breath.**

Like the cherubim, our prophetic kids will be in such a close position to God as to feel the blowing of His breath upon their faces.

"I looked and saw a windstorm coming out of the
north…**an immense cloud with flashing lightning
and surrounded by brilliant light.** The center of the
fire looked like glowing metal, and in the fire
looked like four living creatures. In appearance
their form was that of a man,
but each of them had four faces and four wings… "
EZEKIEL 1:4-6 NIV

This word, "**bright cloud**" is sometimes used
interchangeably with the word, "**overshadow**" when
speaking of the power of Holy Spirit. The bright
cloud that enveloped the disciples on the mountain
of transfiguration, the overshadowing of Mary when
the Holy Ghost came upon her to conceive Jesus
and the power radiating from Peter's healing
shadow all emanated from the same bright glory
cloud Ezekiel saw.

"The Holy Spirit will come upon you,
and the **power of the Most High
will overshadow you [like a shining cloud]** … "
LUKE 1:35,37 AMPLIFIED

"… they brought forth the sick into the streets,
and laid them on beds and couches, that at the **least
the shadow of Peter passing by
might overshadow some of them.**"
ACTS 5:15 KJ

"… **a bright cloud overshadowed (epiakiazo) them:
and behold a voice out of the cloud…** "
MATTHEW 17:5 KJ

"**Epiakiazo**," # 1982 means to envelop in a haze
of brilliancy like the glory cloud; to invest with
divine power and influence.

Our prophetic kids will be overshadowed by the same glory cloud Ezekiel encountered and heaven's agenda will open to them. They will hear the voice of the Lord and the power of the Most High will overshadow them as they move in creative miracles. And like Mary, they will birth the seemingly impossible.

Come take a ride with me as we search God's wisdom on raising prophetic kids. Learn with me how to break gridlocks and deterrents blocking their heart of worship. **It's never too late to protect what God has entrusted to us... He is always right on time... so let's soar the skyways of heaven, hand in hand, as we learn of His amazing ways.**

CHAPTER THREE

*M*AKING OF THE PROPHET, SAMUEL

Earth Blesser

*T*he book of Samuel is a Biblical template for raising prophetic kids. The story begins with barren Hannah crying out to Lord for a child. She was not asking for an ordinary child out of a woman's natural desire for children. But, her grief over the defiled culture compelled her to cry out for a reformer—a son that would uproot idolatry.

> "By giving me a son, I'll give him completely, unreservedly to you. I'll set him apart for a life of holy discipline."
> *I SAMUEL 1:11 THE MESSAGE*

Her prophetic eyes saw the looming demise of Israel if they continued to dishonor God's covenant. It was her answered prayers, just a humble, beseeching woman that actually shifted a cycle of pollution back to one of holiness. God answered Hannah because she was aligned with His heart—He literally prayed His prayers through her.

The original intention of God has always been to make His children "earth blessers." This consuming desire of His heart has never wavered. When God first called Abram, He called him to be a blessing and you know we are the sons of Abraham with that same calling to be "earth blessers."

> "I will make of you a great nation, and I will bless you [with abundant increase of favors] and make your name famous and distinguished, and you will be a blessing [dispensing good to others]...
> **and in you shall all families of the earth be blessed."**
> *GENESIS 12:2,3 AMPLIFIED*

Embracing this responsibility to prepare our children to bless the earth is the first step in raising a prophetic child. Without our foresight and inspiration our children might forfeit their inheritance as "earth blessers" and chase after that which can never satisfy. We as parents must touch their imagination to visualize their DNA encoded with greatness. This challenge will enliven them to their very core.

God chose Abraham as the one man he could depend on to build His dream of blessing all nations. Why? Because **God knew He could trust**

Abraham to teach and command his children in the ways of the Lord.

> "For I know him, that he will **command (tsawah)**
> his children and his household after him, and
> they shall keep the way of the Lord... "
>
> *Genesis 18:19 KJ*

The Hebrew word for "**command**" is #6680, "**tsawah**." It literally means to **anoint**, decree or **cause to exist**. This **command** is unique in that it guarantees a certain type of feedback. Contained within this "**tsawah**," is a deep, heart-felt response— a burning sentiment, not cold or heartless. God guarantees this **command, "tsawah"** will ignite passion and fervor for Him. When decreed, it contains within itself the power to fulfill itself within our kids.

When we dare command our children in the ways of the Lord, then God pledges Himself as our warranty, our indemnity against loss or damage in their lives. God is trusting us to insure the right heart attitude in our children, anointing them with holiness.

Wow! Parents, let's rejoice at the great honor to shape our children's heart. We are equipped to infuse their hearts with His desires and passions. Only then, will they be satisfied with His rich, divine perfections—rising up with apostolic authority in what ever area they are called.

> "A little one shall become a thousand
> and a small one a strong nation:
> I the Lord will hasten it in His time."
>
> *ISAIAH 60:22 KJ*

Like Samuel, our kids will be energized by this holy calling as they lock into their destiny vision. The nations they are called to will surface as we watch their passions develop. Remember, a nation is not just a country but also refers to different people groups such as Hollywood, media, technology, fashion, NFL, education, etc. If we keep our kids free, passionate and soaked in His Spirit, they will playfully and majestically unfold their destiny right before our eyes as we focus on their great worth.

Like Hannah, **we can see our children as an answer to satisfy God's desire.** As we acquaint them with God's fiery glory, their ear will awaken to His heart. Like Hannah, our prophetic eyes will affect their passion to bless the nations.

Make a Smile

I remember when my girls were young, we spent hours browsing the pages of old National Geographic magazines their grandfather had given us. These graphic pictures of suffering humanity touched their young hearts with a desire to bless the nations. There was one particularly impactful story on how Sudanese children spent their entire days gathering cow dung patties. This dung was the sole source of their existence in a barren land. They shielded blistering desert winds in smelly, make-shift shelters pasted together from the cow patties. They scavenged cooking fuel from the treasured dung splattered on the parched ground. Smokey, suffocating fumes drifted in the night air as the dung burned under the infected cooking pot. These children's bodies reeked with the stench of dung… their tiny frames labored in feces… slept in feces… ate feces-laced food, day after monotonous day, with no way of escape.

It was stories like this that impacted my girl's imaginations with visions of themselves as an answer to such hopeless depravity. **Their hearts began bursting with joy for the blessings entrusted to them. Surely, they were determined to be an "earth blesser."**

More recently around Christmas time, I read a colorful catalogue from the ministry, "World Vision," with my three year old granddaughter, Abby. She was captivated by pictures of children with swollen, wormy bellies, carrying buckets of dirty water totted on tiny shoulders. Yet, there were other happy faces hugging baby goats that had been donated as gifts to provide milk in their scanty existence. What made the difference; why did some have smiles? She was full of questions as to why their bellies were swollen and where were their mommies and daddies? She began to imagine their plight as she studied their gaunt faces. One was cuddling a fluffy baby chick.

"That one, Grandma, will she have eggs for breakfast soon?" Her tender heart was engulfed with a passion to, as she put it, "make a smile." "Could we make a smile grandma," she questioned?

Just at the thought of giving, her heart swelled with thankfulness as heaven's gates swung open, flooding her with God's great mercy. Her heart's capacity to love expanded that night and her gratitude for God's goodness in her life spilled over into heartfelt joy. She had her first taste of being an "earth blesser" that magical night.

CHAPTER FOUR

---⟨∞⟩---

THE ARK OF HIS PRESENCE

"How lovely are Your tabernacles, O Lord
of hosts! My soul yearns, yes, even pines and is
homesick for the courts of the Lord; my heart
and flesh cry out and sing for joy to the
living God. Yes, the sparrow has found a house,
and the swallow a nest for herself,
where she may lay her young... even Your altars,
O Lord of hosts, my King and my God."
PSALM 84:1-3 AMPLIFIED

Like the Psalmist, Hannah's heart was to lay her
young Samuel on the altar of the Lord. When her
promised son was born, she nursed him until he was
weaned, then faithful to her vow, brought him to
the Temple at two or three. Samuel's earliest
memories must be of God's tangible presence which
at that time resided in the Ark in the Tabernacle at
Shiloh.

"When she had weaned him, she took him
with her, and brought Samuel to the Lord's house
in Shiloh. The child was growing."
1 SAMUEL 1:24 AMPLIFIED

She knew well His lovely Tabernacle and
yearned to lay her young Samuel on the altar of her
God. Her Spirit continually watched over Samuel
as every year when she came to worship, she
brought him a little robe that she had handmade.

Home school for me was like the little robe
Hannah made for Samuel. It was my way of
watching over my "Samuels," making sure they lay
by the Ark of His presence. Hannah's anointed
mantle clothed Samuel in a prophetic declaration
that he would surely revive Israel.

Like Joseph's coat fashioned by His father,
Isaac, we too can transfer generational mantles,
securing the perpetual flow of the anointing to our
children. Joseph's coat was multi colored and
speaks of the anointing. The Hebrew word,
"mashach" for "anoint" means to paint with many
colors. Joseph's coat was a prophetic picture of his
intended destiny, that he would spread the
anointing and reveal the divine perfections of His
God in idolatrous Babylon.

"Moreover, **his mother made him a little robe**
and brought it to him from year to year… "
1 SAMUEL 2:19 AMPLIFIED

Young Samuel, drawn to the Lord, stayed by
the flickering light of the Temple lamp, choosing to
serve and sleep in the Holy Place, day and night.
However, Eli the Priest's eyesight was dim so that

he could not see, speaking of his darkened insight. Eli, the humdrum, stale clergy, lay down in his own place indifferent to the place of God's presence. **Samuel is a forerunner of prophetic kids in the making that will be "breakers," crushing the religious spirit lurking in the halls of Christendom. There is a shift coming, a wind of change beginning to blow. We must set our children's sail to catch this wind of His Spirit.**

"Samuel ministered to the Lord... The word of the Lord was rare and precious in those days: there was no frequent or widely spread vision.
At that time Eli, whose eyesight had dimmed so that he could not see,
was lying down in his own place.
The lamp of God had not yet gone out in the temple of the Lord, where the ark of God was, and Samuel was lying down.
When the Lord called, Samuel!
And he answered. Here I am."
1 SAMUEL 3:1-3 AMPLIFIED

Hearing God's Voice
———◌〇◌———

Our call is to position our kids before the Ark where they will hear the Lord's voice. **Notice that the first step in hearing God's voice was for Samuel to be obedient to what he thought was Eli's voice.** Eli's voice represented the voice of parental authority in his life and had Samuel not inconvenienced himself to get up out of bed in the middle of night to answer what he thought was Eli's call, then he would have never heard God's voice. That's why it is imperative to raise our children to quickly obey our voices and not allow "stalling" which encourages delayed obedience which is really disobedience. What if Samuel had been too sleepy to get up in that night and obey what he thought was Eli's voice? Would God's voice have slipped away? We cannot allow our children to avoid eye contact or ignore us only to walk away pretending they don't hear us. We're setting up patterns that will muffle their spiritual hearing as well.

"And the Lord called Samuel the third time.
And he went to Eli and said,
Here I am for you did call me.
Then Eli perceived that the Lord was calling the boy. So Eli said to Samuel, Go, lie down.
And if He calls you, you shall say,
Speak, Lord, for your servant is listening.
So Samuel went and lay down in his place."
1 SAMUEL 3:8,9 AMPLIFIED

Samuel had to learn how to hear God's voice by first listening to his voice of authority, Eli.

This should be our children's immediate heart's response, "speak, Mommy, Daddy… for your child is listening." It is then their ears will awaken to God's voice as they obey our voice. This is close to God's heart and has many dimensions.

I remember when He spoke clearly, "Jeri, listen to your child's voice as intently as you would to Mine." They're speaking their heart if you only have an ear to hear! Here is a Truth that unlocks access to their passions.

Jesus was even obedient to death on the cross. He only said what He heard His Father say and did what he saw His Father do. Irreverent, nonchalant, disrespectful worship can darken our kid's spiritual zeal. Tall order I know, but holy obedience is sacred to Jesus.

"As obedient children, let yourselves be pulled
into a way of life shaped by God's life,
a life energetic and blazing with holiness.
God said, I am holy, you be holy."
1 PETER 1:16 THE MESSAGE

"Who shall go up into the mountain of the Lord?
Or who shall stand in His Holy Place?
He who has clean hands and a pure heart... "
PSALM 24:3,4 AMPLIFIED

Paramount is teaching our kids to revere God's presence—sensitizing them to His holiness and ever watchful nearness. **We can cry out for inventive ways to inspire our kids with fathoms of lavish love for Him. For to know Him, is to surely love Him in piercing devotion.**

Staying close to the Ark of His presence, Samuel grew as a visionary. He trusted the smoldering flame would not extinguish under his watch. His prophetic eyes stoked the flame of the Lord, no matter how flickering the lamp burned. These young prophets we are raising are fiery, passionate types that must live closest to the glory. Only in the Holy Place is there enough fire to kindle their divine destiny. **They are destined to be set ablaze with the burning incense of worship.**

I remember reading about Ruth Ward Heflin's humble, yet glorious childhood. Her makeshift home was a few converted Sunday school rooms in her pioneering Pentecostal parent's church. Out of necessity after school, the church prayer meetings were held in her bedroom. Holy Spirit coaxed her sentiments there as she lingered in the charged atmosphere dropping eternal sounds of glory into her young Spirit. It was here, in her quasi church/bedroom, that she touched the eternal realm where anything becomes possible. It was these childhood memories of heaven's sound that later kept her as she traveled the world spreading His glory. **Our homes can literally become a celestial sanctuary.**

Apothecary Anointing

As we ignite a holy fire on the altars of our children's hearts—worship rises. In the Temple, a fire burned on the altar of incense in the Holy Place, typifying a heart of continual worship. The boy prophet Samuel is a type of this sacrificial worshiper. His heart was groomed amid the smoky, fragrant incense and flame of the Lord. Likewise, we can groom our children in the nuances of the Holy Place.

The priests were actually apothecaries, perfumers that gathered and mixed the costly, fragrant spices that burned before the Lord's nostrils. Every morning and evening they would tend the candle stick to keep the flame burning. While trimming the wicks and filling the lamps with oil, the Priest would burn incense on the golden altar before the veil. As he lit his prepared crushed spices, his sacrifice was like gasoline hitting fire and the fragrant, pungent smoke, drifted beneath the curtain, filling the Holy of Holies, where the Lord promised to meet with him.

These precious gums and spices the Priest gathered and crushed for incense cost him everything. There were rare and some only grew in distant, difficult places, often behind enemy territory. One of the sacred gums he gathered as it fell like great drops of tears, oozing from a wounded, bleeding branch. Another fragrant bark he hand-stripped and peeled from a bush until it lay naked. Yet, another sacred spice he scraped from gnarled roots embedded deep in the cavern of hellish places. As His priests our kids must learn the art of the apothecary!

Joseph is a prophetic picture of a fragrant offering before the Lord. This perfume cost him everything and was gathered at a great price. He was abducted by a marauding caravan trading spices. They pirated his holy visionary dream; attempting to loot his legacy of an "earth blesser." The devil thinking he had hijacked Joseph's destiny, imprisoned him in hellish places, but it was here, ironically, that he gathered costly spices to ignite for the Lord's pleasure even while captured by Egypt's cruel bondage. King David, the great singing prophet, also tasted this hardship as he offered the bitter with the sweet, and pledged not to sacrifice to the Lord that which cost him nothing. **We must infuse our kids with the "apothecary anointing," perfumers that prepare lavish sweet-smelling fragrances of spicy incense that wafts before His holy face.**

As we lay our children beside the ark of God's presence, they must know what a great price it will cost to walk in His anointing. Our kid's prophetic journey may lead into dark, hellish, purifying places. Their motives will lay exposed and naked before the Lord—their hidden agendas peeled and stripped. Their soul bleed as drops of tears ooze from their unjust wounding. Just as Joseph's jealous brothers sold his prophetic voice into slavery, so will the enemy try to silence our kid's dreams.

Our young prophets must buttress their character, knowing cleansing and persecution may come.

Remember though, Joseph eventually was made second in command of the most powerful nation of all the known earth. He truly became an "earth blesser" as he spared his people from famine and salvaged the jewel of God's heart, the Jewish people. He ruled in divine justice and truth as he was given the signet ring of Pharaoh's authority. **Great is the reward of the apothecary anointing!**

"Then Pharaoh said to Joseph,
see, I have set you over all the land of Egypt.
And Pharaoh took off his [signet] ring from his
hand and put it on Joseph's hand, and arrayed him
in [official] vestments of fine linen
and put a gold chain about his neck."
GENESIS 41:41,42 AMPLIFIED

CHAPTER FIVE

---⌒⌒---

"STRANGE FIRE"

Irreverence for Holiness

---⌒⌒---

Samuel is a forerunner of prophetic kids—
"breakers" that will crush the religious spirit lurking
in the halls of Christendom. For we see, Eli's two
sons, Hophni and Phinehas were apostate priests in
the Temple where Samuel ministered.

> "The sons of Eli were base and worthless;
> they did not **know (yada)** or regard the Lord."
> *I SAMUEL 2:12 AMPLIFIED*

The word used for **"know"** is **"yada,"** # 3045 in
Strong's Concordance. **"Yada"** means to **know by
experience** and **understand with the eyes of the
heart**. **"Yada"** is often used to express the **intimacy
as only known between a husband and wife**. **"Yada"**

can also mean to be intimately acquainted with or **know "face to face."**

Obviously Eli's sons were casually acquainted with the Lord, because they had grown up in the Tabernacle as young priests, yet they failed to know Him "face to face." Their darkened eyes preyed upon God's power and prostituted His glory for prideful, selfish gain. Because they deceived God in a hypocritical, anemic relationship, they themselves were deceived and presumed they were invincible.

Because they presumptuously took the ark of God's presence into a battle against the Philistines, their nonchalant attitude for holiness caused the glory to depart— "Ichabod." Even though they shouted with such a great earth shaking shout, God refused to answer their cry and the ark was captured.

"…all Israel raised such a great shout
that the ground shook …
hearing the roar the Philistines were afraid …
yet the ark of God was captured
and Eli's two sons, Hophni and Phinehas, died."
1 SAMUEL, 4:5,7,11 NIV

Why? All because Eli neglected to discipline his children and infuse a passion for holy living. 30,000 Israeli soldiers, their father Eli and his sons died that day under the hollow sound of their thunderclap shout, as God stood silent.

Affections of the Heart

Another example of this disregard for holiness is Nadab and Abihu. They offered strange and unholy fire in the wilderness, even after the God of Israel had physically manifested Himself to them in His glory. **God gave them all—His very best and yet it was not enough to hold their affection.**

> "… they (Nadab and Abihu) saw the God of Israel
> [that is, a convincing manifestation of
> His presence], and under His feet it was
> like pavement of bright sapphire stone,
> like the very heavens in clearness."
> *EXODUS 24:9,10 AMPLIFIED*

Experiencing God is not enough; divine encounters are not enough, but it is the issue of our kid's heart that sets the flow of their life! We must be watchmen on the walls of their hearts, guarding their affections and repelling attractions that seduce impure passions. Let's not let, even good things, like sports, internet, friends, etc. arouse more excitement than their passion for Jesus. The things to which they are zealously attached… their heart attitudes and valued sentiments map the future course of their lives. They must offer pure, costly, reverent worship from a repentant, humble heart.

> "Keep vigilant watch over your heart;
> that's where life starts."
> *PROVERBS 4:23 THE MESSAGE*

> "Above all else, guard your affections.
> For they influence everything else in your life."
> *PROVERBS 4:23 TLB*

We must jealously guard their affections, routing out seducing idols that cloud their intimacy with the Lord—for "strange fire" smokes their soul with the spirit of the world. Sowing to the flesh always reaps corruption bringing spiritual death.

> "And Nadab and Abihu, the sons of Aaron,
> each took his censer and put fire in it, and
> put incense on it, and offered **strange (zur)** and
> unholy fire before the Lord, as He had not
> commanded them. And there came forth fire
> from before the Lord and killed them,
> and they died before the Lord."
> *LEVITICUS 10:1,2 AMPLIFIED*

The Hebrew word for **"strange"** is **"zur,"** #2114 in Strong's Concordance. Its root meaning is **nonacquaintance of or unrelatedness.** It speaks of **irreverence for God's presence** and a **nonchalantness to His Holiness.** Guarding the affections of our kid's will stoke the fire on the altar of their heart in fiery intimacy.

CHAPTER SIX

———⟨∞⟩———

$\mathcal{D}$EFYING THE SPIRIT OF
THE WORLD

$\mathcal{S}$hamefully, we are in a culture that demands we accept and validate aberrant behavior without repentance. This luke warmness for sin has crept into our churches. Our society drives a Cross-less religion, a Christianity stripped of the Blood that journeys along the "all paths" lead to God lie. The latest spew of Satan's strategic mind control is the diabolic concept of "COEXIST!" Perhaps you've seen the flood of bumper stickers and celebrity endorsements of the acronym, "COEXIST!" that spells out "C," the crescent moon symbol of Islam; "O," the peace sign for nuclear disarmament/anti war; "E," the "omkar," a supposed primordial sound uttered at creation and now chanted in New Age meditation; "X," the Star of David for Judaism; "I," the Wicca/Pagan Universalist religion and "S," for Yin Yang-Taoism/Confucianism. Finally, they include the "T" symbol of the Christian Cross right along side the others and next to the "!," the ancient phallic symbol for sex goddesses.

And then of course, their politically correct propaganda is, let's be fair minded and embrace all beliefs as one. Oh my, what "strange fire" longs to burn on the altar of our children's hearts in this depraved culture. Oh, the astounding depth of this, "I'm OK, you're OK" mind set—this interfaith solidarity movement indoctrinating our youth with inclusive tolerance for all beliefs and lifestyle choices.

I still remember my favorite homeroom teacher in grade school teaching me that every religion has a Bible of their own, for instance Islam has their Koran. He went on to say they were all sacred... all contained truth! As a fourth grader with no spiritual covering at home, this deception slithered right into my heart. I had been trying to read the Bible on my own as a nine year old, but I remember right at that moment I checked out, dismissing the Bible as just another man's opinion. How could I find Truth when everyone had their own opinions, with one as valid as the other? Even children are searching for absolutes. We must help them find their way through the maze of mistruths hand fed them, often by those they admire the most.

Cain fell prey to this same ancient spirit of bloodless sacrifice void of the cross of Christ. When his offering didn't get God's approval, Cain lost his temper and went into a rage. Sound familiar? When our kids challenge the confines of a crucified life and behave outside the bounds of holiness... we must help them master their lower nature.

God spoke to Cain. "Why this tantrum?
Why the sulking? If you do well, won't you be
accepted? And if you don't do well,
sin is lying in wait for you, ready to pounce;
it's out to get you, you've got to master it."
GENESIS 4:6 THE MESSAGE

These same impure waters of, "doing things my way," then demanding God endorse it have polluted the nations through out the ages. Ancient spirits never die, they just repackage themselves to be culturally relevant. Even Israel, the apple of God's eye, succumbed to Asherah, who instituted male prostitutes and sodomites in her divine court. She seduced worshipers in every unholy passion and depraved appetite.

She self-titled herself, the "Queen of Heaven" and called herself, "Qudshu" translated, "The Holy One" or "Holiness." This deified queen was worshiped as the incarnation of the Holy Spirit. Her very name means "habitation" and a dove adorns her headdress. Interestingly, Los Angeles is named after her—City of the Queen of Angels.

"They threw out everything God, their God,
had told them, and replaced Him with two
statue-gods shaped like bull-calves and
then a phallic pole for the whore goddess Asherah.
They worshiped cosmic forces, sky gods and
goddesses, and frequented the sex-and-religion
shrines of Baal. They even sank so low as to offer
their own sons and daughters as sacrificial burnt
offerings! They indulged in all the black arts of

magic and sorcery. In short they prostituted themselves to every kind of evil available to them. And God had had enough."

2 KINGS 17: 16,17 THE MESSAGE

"They took up with other gods, fell in with the ways of life of the pagan nations... they did all kinds of things on the sly, things offensive to their God, then openly and shamelessly built local sex-and-religion shrines at every available site."

2 KINGS 17;7-9 THE MESSAGE

The religious spirit and immorality are two sides of one coin, where you find one, you will find the other. Our one true God is holy and demands holy living. We must insulate our kids from the impure spew promulgated from Hollywood gurus, the media moguls and the sewer of internet soliciting. Statistics tell us with in a decade over 10 billion youth—not million, will be addicted to internet porn.

"Come I'll show you the judgment of the great Whore who sits enthroned over many waters, the Whore with whom the kings of the earth have gone whoring, show you the judgment on earth dwellers drunk on her whorish lust."

REVELATION 17:1,2 THE MESSAGE

This great whore of Babylon is not a bride but a prostitute who lures unsuspecting kids with the entrapping bait of the supposed "intimacy," her lusting love falsely offers. She assures her victims that salvation, coupled with loose sex is acceptable. Her love is for hire without covenant and non-exclusive. Only the love of God and intimacy with precious Holy Spirit can resist her vile seductions.

Only the power of the blood and the name of Jesus will loose her charming, yet deceitfully ravenous claws.

> "… Eli's sons were ripping off the people
> and sleeping with the women who
> helped out in the sanctuary."
> *1 SAMUEL 2:22 THE MESSAGE*

Sound familiar? They sinned blatantly right in the Presence of God. Our statistics and the worlds are no different. This has to change! Eli's son's presumed they were above God's judgment and desecrated their holy calling. So now when they called upon the Lord, He knew them not. This was a far cry from Samuel's voice that God always honored. Unholiness annuls apostolic authority and mocks God's command to take dominion in the earth. We must wake up to the seducing spirits released in this hour, entrapping our kids. There is a rampant church doctrine that disfigures "God's Grace" and licenses sin under the guise of His great mercy. In truth, glory is the realization of the full working of God's Grace played out in a holy life lived through Jesus' shed blood.

We must shoot straight with our kids and tell them the dire consequences of unrepentant fornication.

> "Now the works of the flesh are manifest, which are
> these… fornication… uncleanness, lasciviousness…
> idolatry … that they which do such things
> shall not inherit the kingdom of God."
> *GALATIANS 5:19,21 KJV*

The weight of our culture is working against us, so we must be extremely alert to protect the garden of our kid's hearts.

Keeping Watch Over
the Garden

Sexual sins are the only sins that inherently carry a curse against our own body. We can see this in the statistics of the health hazards of promiscuity. **Indisputably, purity must be instilled in our kids as a prerequisite for holiness. One precludes the other!** Sin and holiness can not live together in the same Temple. **Satan is on a tirade slithering through God's virgin soil, disqualifying our youth from holy purposes.** We must oust him from the garden of our child's heart, irrevocably! One of the first commands of God is to protect and keep His garden.

> "And the Lord God took the man and put him
> in the Garden of Eden to **dress (avadh)** it
> and to **keep (shamar)** it."
> *GENESIS 2:15 KJ*

The Hebrew word for dress is **"avadh,"** #5647. One translation renders it as, **to serve God in an exhilarating experience without fatigue or bondage or to cause to worship as a holy priest.** The Hebrew word for keep is **"shamar,"** #8104, translated: **to guard, keep or to watch over as an intercessor—to be a watchman.** This is why God chose Abraham to fulfill His promises for He knew Abraham would be a watchman over his children.

It has to do with **careful attention paid to the obligations of a covenant.**

"For I know him (Abraham), that he will command his children and his household after him, and they shall **keep (shamar)** the way of the Lord...
GENESIS 18:19 KJ

Unholiness is contagious but holiness is not contagious. In other words, our kids can not become holy by association, yet they can be contaminated be unholy relationships and touching unclean things. **Holiness is not infectious but unholiness is infectious. (Haggai 2:12) We see here it is much easier to be polluted that to stay holy!**

We are commanded to honor God with our body. If we want blessed kids, we must guard them from the "snakey," twisted hiss of our perverted culture.

"Flee from sexual immorality. All other sins a man commits are outside his body, but he who sins sexually sins against his own body. Do you not know that your body is a temple of the Holy Spirit, who is in you, whom you have received from God? You are not your own; you were bought at a price. Therefore honor God with your body."
1 CORINTHIANS 6:18,19 NIV

Who may ascend the hill of the Lord?
Who may stand in his holy place?
He who has clean hands and a pure heart... "
PSALM 24:3,4 NIV

We can not allow our children to burn "strange fires" on the altars of their hearts. Sacrifice literally means, "that which is brought near." Sacrifice must literally be interwoven with a holy life—its very fibers—a gift of their very own lives. As their worship is consumed, the vapors of their Spirit and sentiments of their hearts are brought before Him. **We must not allow our kids to overlook their highest privilege and honor, that of approaching a Holy God with a pure heart.**

I remember being in a friend's home when she disciplined, her 4 year old son and he responded to his mother, "I rebuke you in the name of Jesus." She was withholding something he wanted so he yielded to the power of witchcraft. Yes, that's right, even a four year old can yield to this type of witchcraft—after all it is a work of the flesh. He had learned of his spiritual authority but hadn't yet been taught to crucify his old man and walk in his new creation.

Snake in the House

"The acts of the sinful nature are obvious:
sexual immorality, impurity and debauchery;
idolatry and **witchcraft**; hatred, discord, jealousy,
fits of rage, selfish ambition, dissensions, factions
and envy; drunkenness, orgies, and the like. I warn
you, as I did before, that those who live like this
will not inherit the kingdom of God."
GALATIANS 5:19-21 NIV

We can't be squeamish with the term, "witchcraft" as the scripture defines it as a work of the flesh... not some demonic force. There is a white witchcraft, without horns and a tail that is listed here, a work of the flesh and demons cannot be held responsible. We must help our kids be accountable for their own fleshly desires. The culprit here is none other than the yielding of our own human will! Even God won't force His love, He so treasures our free will. He will have us love Him by choice! He knows quite well, that, "He can't make some one love Him."!

Unfortunately, it is common to hear kids screaming at parents, "I hate you," "Leave me alone," etc. It's become pretty much the norm in homes to normalize strife, tolerate sibling bickering and arguing. Temper tantrums are nothing more than a work of our kid's flesh called **"rage"** in Galatians 5. **When we allow envy and strife in our homes, we're putting out a welcome mat inviting every evil work to come on in.**

> **"For where there is envying and strife is, there is confusion and every evil work."**
> *JAMES 3:16 KJ*

I get prayer requests from so many mothers, saying they are having panic attics, insomnia, suicidal thoughts, debilitating depression, confusion, etc. Could it be, "a snakey" intruder has been invited in? A hissing spirit of "strife" may have surreptitiously slithered in."

Our kid's are crying out for help to control their flesh. They are young and naïve, needing strong, clear boundaries to guard Holy Spirit's influence.

Kids have amazing spiritual insight at a very young age. I remember the amusing story of three year old Cory. Her mother spied a crumpled, half-empty sack of marsh mellows tucked in the kitchen cabinet.

Cory, she asked, "why did you disobey and eat the marsh mellows?"

Cory proudly stated, "no mommy, I obeyed my Holy Spirit. He told me He wanted a marsh mellow."

It was quite cute and amusing at the time, but down the road, nothing makes kids happier than being obedient.

I remember a special time with my grand daughter when our joy was intoxicating—overflowing.

"Grandma, hasn't it been the most beautiful day? I feel so happy inside—I just wish we could be stuck together forever—or have a secret door between our houses."

Thinking back, I knew why Abby and I were feeling so "fully alive." We had been learning how to let our Spirit man be in charge. She was lov'n it and so was I. Children feel especially satisfied and good about themselves when their Spirit man is in charge.

We must stomp the snake if he gets in the house—rebellion, stubbornness and strife have to go.

I remember a funny story when we lived in the country. Our German Shepherd, Homer, loved to sniff out rattle snakes. When we heard his "snake howl," we knew he had one cornered. My husband jumped up in the middle of the night in his underwear and threw on some cowboy boots for protection. I flipped on the flood lights to see the most amusing sight of my husband with his bare legs in cowboy boots doing major damage to that snake. Anyway, if we could only be that brutal when it comes to beheading spiritual snakes that slither in our homes.

> "For rebellion is as the sin of witchcraft, and stubbornness is idolatry... "
> *1 SAMUEL 15:22 AMPLIFIED*

Lovers of the Truth

As we lay our "Samuels" beside the ark of His presence, He saturates them with the fruits of Holy Spirit.

> "But the fruit of the [Holy] Spirit [**the work which His presence within accomplishes**] is love, joy (gladness), peace, patience (an even temper, forbearance), kindness, goodness (benevolence), faithfulness, gentleness, (meekness, humility), self-control (self-restraint, continence)...
> *GALATIANS 5:22,23 AMPLIFIED*

Esau is an Old Testament type of a fleshly, carnal man. The fruits didn't grow and he caved in to his flesh. (Genesis 25:34) Despising his birthright, he sold it for a fleeting pleasure, dishonoring his priestly position. As the first born, Esau was ordained as the family priest that safe guarded the generational blessing and preserved the

Abrahamic covenant to be an "earth blesser." And though he later wept bitterly for his squandered inheritance, he had irretrievably forfeited his blessing.

> **"Watch out for the Esau syndrome: trading away God's lifelong gift in order to satisfy a short-term appetite.** You well know how Esau later regretted that impulsive act and wanted God's blessing… but by then it was too late, tears or no tears."
> *HEBREWS 12:16,17 THE MESSAGE*

We must impress our kids with the severity of their choices. We must stake them to His Truth, just as young saplings are staked to insure they grow up straight and tall, not crooked or bent. It is only the love of Truth that will keep our kids free from the spew of deception coming in these last days.

One of the most damaging lies permeating our culture is the humanistic concept of "time out" as a way of correcting children. This counterfeit concept of "time out" is helpless to drive out foolishness bound in their heart and is not mentioned in Scripture. Consider reading my first book, "The Perfect Heart" which lays down a line by line foundation for Godly parenting.

I remember as a young mother, I had determined to never spank my children as the idea was abhorrent to me. The scars of my own childhood abuse tainted my understanding of loving Biblical discipline.

But thank God for an up front friend that confronted me, "You know, you are emotionally abusing your toddler by letting your temper flare when she is out of control and then withdrawing your affection."

It was true, I found myself saying hurtful things and distancing my heart when she overwhelmed my stretched nerves. I realized I had exalted my painful childhood abuse above God's wisdom. The lie is— Godly discipline is not abuse but proves our love for that child. My hurtful past had spawned deception! Thankfully, quick alignment came as I began to love the Truth of God's Word concerning Biblical child training.

> **"... God will send them strong delusion,**
> **that they should believe a lie because**
> **they loved not the Truth... "**
> *2 THESSALONIANS 2:10,11 PARAPHRASED*

When we deceive God, we deceive ourselves! Strong delusion is rarely traceable as the very concept of "deception" means we don't see we are being misled. God will allow us to live a lie and feel good about it, if we so choose.

We must rivet our kid's heart to God's written Truth, His Bible. You know, one of the definitions of Satan is, "one that stands between." He is an ancient master—causing static on the airwaves of our heart. He slanders the Word of God relegating it to irrelevant, unsuitable and up for debate. Yet in actuality, God's truth is ageless wisdom flowing from the Ancient of Days. For it is loving His Truth that alone crowns us with beauty and dignity.

Above all else, let's cuddle up and embrace God's "Love Letter" with our kids. I promise, nothing else can touch the ecstasy of being His Fire

Bride. It's upon this foundation alone that we will become passionate lovers of His Truth. This must be our daily heart's cry!

> "Let me see Your face,
> let me hear Your voice,
> For your voice is soothing
> and Your face is ravishing."
> *SONG OF SONGS 2:14 THE MESSAGE*

CHAPTER SEVEN

ℴ𝒩o Applause

Just Ran Out of Time

ℋannah was ridiculed for her zeal and even rebuked by the high priest, Eli. As she wept, crying out for a "breaker" child, Eli accused her of being drunk. He was clueless that Hannah was in the birth pangs of delivering Samuel, a reformer Prophet that would revive the dead priesthood back to holiness. It's rare that we will get any praise for raising prophetic kids—I guarantee, the world's system will not congratulate us. But like Hannah, we can still commit, despite painful harassment, to raise Godly children.

As a young mother, I remember visiting a chapel service in our daughter's Christian school. I was sitting in the back as a guest and found myself deeply grieved at what I saw. Some kids were squirming in their chairs doodling ink cartoon figures on their neighbor's arms. Others giggled at a flirtatious boy, as he flipped his dangling bangs with a hair comb. Others slumped in boredom as they sulked impatiently for the drone to end. They were all pretty much oblivious to the Lord's presence. How could this be? I knew most of these kids and they knew better. Their parents were our church friends. It was then that I heard the Lord speak, "bring them home."

I was shocked! He couldn't be asking this of me. As I wrestled with the idea, a vision rolled across my mind. There it was! I saw my self standing before God's throne making excuses of why I hadn't imparted my daughters with certain Godly precepts.

Then like hollow words resounding in an empty cavern I heard myself saying, **"but Lord, I just ran out of time… I just ran out of time… I intended to… but I just ran out of time."**

I ranted on and on until the gavel of His judgment slammed down and the case was closed. I knew then that I must follow His plan never looking back.

25 years ago home schooling was fringe and mostly something missionaries did out of necessity. But my heart began to surge with passion for God's will.

All I wanted was to stand before Him and hear Him say, "Well done my good and faithful daughter." For me, that meant homeschooling, which I must admit I learned to love with a passion.

After all, I didn't want any, "buts" when I stood before the Lord. The next years were ones of brow beating, brain washing, family interrogations, indoctrinations, and fear tactics. You name it, I took the heat. But the devil is a liar and today my blessings overtake me on every wave.

Honoring Your Sons Above God

Interestingly, God exalted Hannah's son, to cleanse the House of God while He rejected the predicted priesthood. Why was Eli's seed disqualified and Hannah's accepted? Wasn't Eli of the royal descent of Aaron, the Levitical Priesthood separated by God? Hadn't he judged Israel, as well for 40 years and shown profound devotion for God? Yet, God judged him and cut off his seed forever. Why? Eli failed to command his sons in the way of the Lord—he tolerated their misbehavior. He judged Israel well but when his own sons sinned, he wouldn't deal with it.

In other words, Eli's ministry looked great on the outside but to God it was most displeasing. The reason being in denial concerning our kid's behavior is so entrapping as it relieves us of responsibility. We must be alert to the false comfort that denial offers. Like the toddler strutting around the room with dirty diapers, everyone knows where the whiff is from but him. We can't be the last to acknowledge our kids need to be cleaned up! Holy Spirit eagerly longs to bring insight. Scripture tells us that Eli failed to do this and honored his sons above God.

> "… you (Eli) honor your sons above Me… "
> *1 SAMUEL 2:29 AMPLIFIED*

How do we honor our children above God? Plainly stated in scripture, Eli did not restrain his sons.

> "… I will judge his house (Eli) forever
> for the iniquity which he knew, because
> his sons made themselves vile, and
> **he restrained (kahah) them not.**"
> *1 SAMUEL 3:13 PARAPHRASED KJ*

The original concept of this word, "**restrain**" is "**kahah,**" #3543 in Hebrew. It means to reproach or scold. Its root means to be feeble and fail in strength. It is often used of a wick burning with very little flame, almost gone out. It also speaks of eyes becoming dim and of a broken down spirit.

Eli did not "restrain" his sons. His discipline was feeble, exerting weak, halfhearted strength. His defiant sons got the upper hand, quenching his flame. Eli's lineage of priests lay smoldering in the ashes of exhausted, good intentions as his sons overstepped his authority

Raising a prophetic child can only be done by the power and strength found in precious Holy Spirit. Only He can equip us for our toughest feat—but, oh, the rewards so soaringly majestic. Some children with strong wills will contend with bitter determination to be the family boss. Their childish disobedience might seem innocent and somewhat playful at the time, but trust me, as we yell, "one—two—three," we are damaging their tender souls as well as bringing pain to the heart of God.

Our role is to "tune" their heart strings to the sound of His voice. Remember, we are training them to listen and respond to our voice as they would the very voice of God. God's voice is delicate and sensitive, so we don't want to misrepresent Him. Properly tuning our kid's ears is precious to the Lord.

God does not yell at His kids! If we're yelling at our kids then, hello—this is a warning siren that discipline is long over due. We are training them to respond to our voice as a forerunner of God's gentle voice. Jesus is not a "handler"—rough or coldhearted. He only touches and leads, never drives or pushes!

Godly discipline requires instant, complete obedience. Delayed obedience is really disobedience and can sometimes mean the difference between life and death. What if Abraham had not been quick to listen when the Lord said, "stay" the knife when he was about to sacrifice Isaac? God suddenly gave new directions…Abraham had to be quick to listen.

What if our child hesitates to obey in a time of danger? That is why early toddler discipline is so crucial as we protect them from danger and their own selfish will before it gains a stronghold. I remember telling my girls the story of Bambi and how she would give just one swish of her tail to signal hunters and her babies would run for cover.

"That's how closely you should watch Mommy," I would tell my girls.

Know this—how our kids treat us is how they will treat precious Holy Spirit later on in life—with respect or disrespect.

What we once thought was just a cute, conniving stage will thrive with age, breaking down our spirit and literally wearing us out in time. How can a toddler break down a parent's spirit? Trust me, it can happen and we'll find ourselves dejected, lifeless—looking to escape this zoo of a, "jungle gym" life! **Whenever we find ourselves irritated with our kids, frustrated and lashing out, then we have passed the time for correcting their attitude.** Children can sense our detachment and our "zoning out." Then rejection sets in, all because we didn't set boundaries for them. The more they feel rejected—the more they "spaz," acting up for attention and the cycle goes on. Their budding hearts are crying out for help in controlling their flesh. If our eyes dim and we lose vision for our Godly responsibility then life becomes so entangled.

Even though Eli was a pious man strongly devoted to the Lord, he was still judged because he was a lax father who lost control over his own sons. Publicly, Eli received honor and notoriety as High Priest but God saw things from a different perspective. He saw Eli missing his generational destiny of raising Godly seed. God is a God of the generations, and can only establish His purposes through the obedience of three generations such as Abraham, Isaac and Jacob. We see the great schism of God's Kingdom when David's son, Solomon, defied his father's devotion of being a man after God's own heart.

"…if you live in my presence as your father David lived, pure in heart and action, living the life I've set out for you, obedient to my guidance and judgments, then I'll back your kingly rule over Israel… but if you or your sons betray me, ignoring my guidance and judgments… I'll repudiate this Temple."
1 KINGS 9:4,5,6 THE MESSAGE

God personally appeared twice to Solomon promising to bless his throne forever, if only Solomon would obey. (1 Kings 9:3-6) He gave him an awesome promise that His eyes and heart would be with him perpetually, if he only obeyed. But even after his third personal visitation from the Lord, Solomon failed to rend his heart, squandered his inheritance and delayed God's plan for a glorious Israel.

"Solomon did evil in the sight of the Lord, and went not fully after the Lord, as David his father did."
1 KINGS 11:6 KJ

Marked for Glory

That is why chapter after chapter in my book, "The Perfect Heart," spells out Biblical patterns for childhood discipline, impartation, creating worship hunger and Holy Spirit intimacy. As these are the foundational stones for the raising of a prophetic child.   Oh Lord, let us not short-circuit our generational purposes ordained of God.

One theme that weaves through out the stories of the Bible is that of God choosing individuals to accomplish His will.   We are so indoctrinated in Christianity to have the "sheep" mentality that says, "baa"… "baa… let's all do this together"   We've been slyly seduced to a "communistic" form of religion.   But, do you know God has always selected sole individuals to spear head his adventures? Didn't the one man Abraham birth an entire nation of God's set apart people?   Didn't one man, David, slew Goliath while an entire army stood watch? Didn't Daniel single handedly confront witchcraft and win over Babylon and its heathen king?   Didn't the lone hand of the Apostle Paul pen most of the New Testament?   Didn't God's hand select the Apostle John to singly and by himself alone prophetically frame the unveiling of the end-times in the book of Revelation.

It is in this legacy that we must crystallize our children's individual destiny for greatness.   They already have His radical DNA surging their being and we must inflame their souls with a tattoo of the signature of God, eternally marking them for His pleasure.

**"…A little one shall become a thousand
and a small one a strong nation"**
ISAIAH 60:22 KJ

This new breed of prophetic kids will surge out of oblivion, perplexing the standardized system.   I recently read of such a young lady who spent her summer vacation, filming under cover in abortion clinics. Posed as a fourteen year old, she exposed illegal activities. She then posted her expose on YouTube, catching the attention of Governors, legislators and even Fox News. With just one thought from God, this teen ager shut down more abortion clinics, instigated more legislation and stopped more funding than all of the protesters before her. These are the reformers, the prophetic kids that God is unleashing in this hour. Let's get excited!

CHAPTER EIGHT

---∞---

*A*POSTOLIC AUTHORITY

Empowered Words

---∞---

*A*mazing as it is, none of Samuel's words fell to the ground—none were unheard or unanswered. God empowered his every word—enforcing what ever he said. Isn't that wild? **How did this young prophet gain such intense communication with God? Simply—he honored and obeyed God's voice, so God reciprocally honored and obeyed Samuel's voice!**

> "Samuel grew; the Lord was with him and let none of his words fall to the ground."
> *1 SAMUEL 3:19 AMPLIFIED*

Oh, the great potential a prophetic kid has to move in this level of governmental authority through the power of their spoken words? Remember, when our kids cherish and obey God's Word then God in turn obeys their words.

It was no different with Jesus who was fully God, yet chose to lay aside His divinity and function solely as a man in absolute obedience to precious Holy Spirit. **He came as an example to demonstrate what a Spirit led man looks like—the glory he would carry.** When Jesus spoke healing, His Father honored and obeyed His words and the sick were healed. It's no different with us. We must believe in the power of our spoken word as we yield to Him. He longs to perform what we say!

Because of the demonic warring powers assigned to earth in this hour, it is crucial this upcoming prophetic generation functions in Kingdom authority. It is ineffective to feed our kids passive, historical Bible stories that lull them as inert spectators. No! These stories must infuse them with power images of who they really are.

Only through face to face encounters, visitations and visionary hero identification will our kids be enlivened. Statistics tell us that over 70% of the typical kid's church diet of David and Goliath coloring pages will leave the Church and never return. They actually become inoculated against any further interest in the Bible as they feel they've heard it all and find it quite like bland pabulum. **They're wired for greatness and if we don't give it to them, they'll find it in the ecstasy of experimenting with fringe benefits the devil offers.**

His Mouthpiece

Joshua experienced this amazing validation of his spoken words when fighting with the Amorites and needed more daylight to finish the battle.

> "… **Joshua said, sun, stand** still upon Gibeon; and moon in the Valley of Ajalon. **And the sun stood still,** and the moon stayed, until the people had avenged themselves upon their enemies. So the sun stood still in the midst of heaven, and hastened not to go down about a whole day. And there was no day like that before it or after it, that **the Lord heeded the voice (qol) of a man.** For the Lord fought for Israel."
> *JOSHUA 10:12,13,14 PARAPHRASED*

Also Elijah also experienced this enforcement of his words when he raised a widow's dead son.

> "And **the Lord heard the voice (qol)** of Elijah, and the soul of the child came back into him again, and he revived."
> *1 KINGS 17:22 AMPLIFIED*

Most often this word, "qol," #6963 in Strong's Concordance is attributed to God's voice. But in the instance of Elijah and Joshua the Lord says He heeded their **voice, their "qol." Imagine that the very word used to describe God's voice, is now describing their voice as well—that's when the miracle happens.**

"Qol's" definition is, "the voice of speech" and the Arabic root meaning is the "impetuous rush of heavy rain." (Jamieson Faussett Brown Commentary) Our voice of speech, like theirs, can release mighty rushes of heavy rain, speaking of the outpouring of Holy Spirit.

One definition for "prophet" is the Hebrew word, "nataf" which means to "drop like rain." This anointing comes from soaking in His presence as a heavy mist until our Spirit is permeated and overflows.

How amazing is it that we are called to be His "mouthpiece"? How humbled we are when prophetic voices are described with the same word, "qol," that Daniel used to describe the precious Lord's voice.

"His body also was like the beryl,
and His face as the appearance of lightning,
and his eyes as lamps of fire,
and his arms and his feet...color to polished brass,
and the **voice (qol)** of his words
like the voice of a multitude."
DANIEL 10:6 KJ

God Talking to God

The Lord heard these Prophet's voices because Holy Spirit inbreathed their request. God was actually praying to God through the prophets yielded Spirit!!! God was responding to Himself through their voice as His "mouthpiece." **God only answers Himself!!!** Their prophetic voice actually releases the intentions of God's will in the earth.

He is looking for those who will echo His heart back to Him. The Spirit of prayer is all about, God talking to God!!!

We've all been frustrated with, "asking anything according to His will and He hears us." (1st John 5:14) But Romans 8:25 tells us that only Holy Spirit knows the mind and will of the Father. **This latter rain, prophetic generation will feel God's heart beat— echoing His will—exhaling His breath. We will be His "breathy blitz,"—His voice in the earth, confounding hell—rushing in the heavy rain of the end times, confounding hell!**

"And they waited for Me as for the rain,
and they opened their mouths wide
as for the spring rain."
JOB 29:23 KJ

The Divine Exhale

We must stir this revelation in our children. We must cultivate their voice to be fueled by His divine exhale? Something must resound in them— reverberate. They must say it is not enough to know the Word, believe the Word and do the Word, but now we must become the voice of the Word. Of course, Jesus is the Word and Holy Spirit His breath but He needs us as His voice in the earth. **There must be a sound in our kid's voice that the Father recognizes as His own. Because God only responds to Himself, He's wanting to copyright their voice—become its owner and producer.** He's jealous to release the sound of His voice in the earth through this prophetic generation. What was Elijah's voice able to do? Give life, subdue witchcraft, open and close the heavens, and more. That same voice reverberates in us!

As the end times approach and demonic hordes are unleashed, we must equip our kid's with spiritual ammunition.

"And take the... sword of the Spirit
which is the word (rhema) of God."
EPHESIANS 6:17 KJ

"Rhema," # 4487 translates in Greek as a **word spoken or uttered by a living voice**; a command of God. It is from a root word, "rheo" meaning to speak. **"Rhema"** is defined as a **God-breathed word; a God word exhaled,** not the written word. This sword of the Spirit is not effective tucked in the sheath of our thoughts but must be released through the **"rhema"** echoed on our holy lips. We must resound His God breathed words, not just His written word. It is then that His God breathed Word is empowered and activated in the earth. His word, released through our mouth is self contained and holds within itself the power to fulfill itself. We must speak and stay silent no longer.

"... Man does not live on bread alone, but on every **word (rhema)** that comes from the mouth of God."
MATTHEW 4:4 NIV

That verse actually translates, **"every word that is continually proceeding from the mouth of God." There is a "now" word—a present truth that we must introduce to our kids. They must be privy to the slightest whisperings of His ever fresh, relevant**

voice. They must expand beyond the "logos," the written scripture and enliven their spirit man to the ever present sound of His voice.

King of the Mountain

⎯⎯⎯⎯ ⌘ ⎯⎯⎯⎯

"For we wrestle not against flesh and blood,
but against **principalities (arche)**, against **powers**,
against the **rulers** of the darkness of the world,
against spiritual wickedness in high places
(or spiritual houses in the heavenlies.)"
EPHESIANS 6:12 PARAPHRASED

The Greek word #746, "**arche**" means someone in authority over a certain territory that has dominion and power. Principality is the state of being first or high in rank. **It is an office of authority—the power of a prince—the offspring of a king.** The clue here is what is the source of the princely power… the prince of the power of the air, Satan, or Prince Jesus, the Son of God? Biblically we think of a principality as an evil power but it can more generally refer to a high ranking authority that's in charge, good or evil. It can speak of someone ruling in dominion over a certain land mass or people group.

Principalities design strategies and schemes to bastion their position while the **powers** are the muscles that execute the plans of the principalities—they always work together in tandem. Rulers seek organizations and groups to embody from which to rule, just as demons embody people in order to control them. Strongholds entrenched by this **"power house trio"** of principalities, powers and rulers manipulate fathers as head of the home all the way up to unions, Federal Reserve, U.N., Czars, etc. The rulers disperse propaganda by twisting deceiving lies into reasonable, fair-minded and intelligent know how. Obviously, this diabolical hierarchy is out to usurp the legitimate headship of Father, Son and Holy Spirit's Kingly Domain!

One **synonym for "principality" is "apostle."** An apostle is the highest ranking office that Jesus gave to His Church. Unfortunately, the religious spirit has pulled off a power grab and instituted its own exclusive club that struts in its own acclaim. But Jesus is restoring this apostolic anointing to individuals, leaders and ministries that He authorizes from heaven, not those self-titled by Church mandates, often void of power. **God is establishing His own "apostolic houses"** to replace ancient rooted, wicked spiritual houses in the heavenlies.

How does this relate to raising prophet kids? **In order to dismantle wicked principality power structures, a Godly societal reformer must penetrate the "power house" effecting change from within.** The most influential change comes from within the **"power house."** For instance, when our new president is elected—he moves into the white house bringing his staff and advisers with him. The old administration is out and policy swiftly changes.

Godly apostolic authority is legitimized in those who rule in princely dominion and Kingdom authority while walking in purity. Too many times, we've seen saints infiltrate Hollywood, politics, etc.

with great, initial influence only to be entangled in the web ruling these **"power houses"**—the tainted saints fall—succumbing to the stronghold's wicked schemes and strategies. Our kids must be clothed with God Himself in order to infiltrate and take ground from these demonic lords.

> **"... the Spirit of the Lord clothed Gideon with Himself and took possession of him... "**
> *JUDGES 6:34 AMPLIFIED*

And we know Gideon tore down his father's altar to Baal, displacing whoring idolatrous ruling spirits. (Judges 6: 25) He evicted the oppressive Midianites who tormented God's people. Daniel, another holy apostle, evacuated ruling spiritual wickedness in Babylon. Apostles are only authorized to tear down from within the evil system. Daniel had to be relocated to Babylon before he could demolish the **"power house trio."** He was fearlessly courageous as he prayed before an open window in defiance of idol worship. He shifted the greatest world empire as a ruling apostle that displaced wicked principalities.

> **"I make a decree that in all my royal dominion men must tremble and fear before the God of Daniel, for He is the living God... "**
> *Daniel 6:26 Amplified*

God is searching the whole earth for someone in whom He can show Himself strong. **Where are the Daniels and the Gideons?** Cry out with me for our prophetic kids to establish holy **"power houses"** in all Kingdom mountains—media, entertainment, religion, government, education, etc.

God is seeking for recruits as there are no vacuums in the heavens—these wicked principalities must be displaced. These ancient King of the Mountains have no intention of vacating. It's time we give them their eviction notice!

Let the true "apostolic houses" legitimized by God Himself rise up and occupy—occupy in geography and demographics—territories and nations—people groups such as, Yale, the U.N., MTV, G7 Summit, Federal Reserve Bank, etc.

I hear the prophetic word of the Lord saying, **"Evacuate, evacuate, evacuate, you dark prince of the air."**

We must equip our kids to be "King of the mountain"—remove the bullies and dislodge ruling powers—saying, "move over, I'm King of this mountain." Hopefully, our prophetic mountain climbers will scale the heights of God's Kingdom and rule from His Holy High Mountain.

The former Russian government had an impure understanding of this principle to instruct children at an early age in their giftings. That's why they won all the gold medals with their gymnasts. Cruelly, they would take young kids with athletic propensity from their homes and board them in rigorous training camps. Not good, but my point is they recognized what young kid's talents were and then focused on making them champions. We can learn from this early discernment of our kid's giftings and focus on their latent potential.

I remember reading the bio of Thomas Edison. When he was kicked out of elementary school, he begged his mother for a makeshift lab in the basement of their home. Enthralled at his new found freedom, he enjoyed experimenting with his creative side. Surely, the hand of the Lord was upon him as he delved into his God given talent. What if his mother had been religious and confined him to conventional methods of education. He was so brilliant that normal school bored him and quenched his fiery quest for break out inventions.

Likewise, the young boy, Albert Einstein, was mesmerized by the sunbeams filtering through the misty haze as he walked to school. These exquisite beams intrigued him as they lit up the morning sky. Later, all of his discoveries were sparked from his inquisitive imagination. It was his childhood dreaming that later broke the hidden codes of physics, unlocking the mysteries of light. **We must slow down and enjoy our kids, as God is truly leading them through their desires and fascinations.**

As we inquire of the Lord as to what He created our kids for, then we'll have divine insight on how to raise them up as, true "apostolic power houses." The Lord is anxious to download this revelation as we spend time with Him. Often, all it takes is just noticing what they love and are passionate about.

You know my daughter, Grace, always begged to play the piano when it came time for Algebra. At first, I didn't know what to think, but the Lord impressed me to let her run with her desires. I figured as long as she can balance a check book it doesn't really matter how she scores on her SAT's.

As only the Lord can, she ended up being awarded a music scholarship at a Christian University, where they waved her achievement scores. Amazing!

My other daughter, Amy, was quite different as she was very scholarly. She would literally ask to buy certain text books and then read them entirely on her own, cover to cover. She would be so enthralled with her books that often she'd just vanish. But, we could always find her off cuddled up with her library stash. She actually came in one day telling me that it was time for her to start college. I remember crying, as it came as such a shock—but I knew it was God. She was only sixteen at the time and later graduated Magna Cum Laude on a President's scholarship. This was so astounding, as we never spent more that a few hours a day in structured home schooling. We had a lot of free time to explore their interests and just be with Him—you know He's every where in every moment—even down by the pond feeding Peeper, our pet duck.

Our house was high on a hill where Peeper slept on the porch between our aging German shepherd's paws to feel safe. Once in a while Homer gave a token growl to protest this uninvited sleeping mate, but normally he just snoozed on. Anyway the pond was quite a bit down the mountain so we would call, Peeper... Peeper and she would take flight, soaring majestically with a spectacular landing right next to us on our row boat seat. Wow! It was in moments like this that we felt God's glory. **Experiencing His glory is sometimes nothing more than feeling "fully alive."** We all giggled that morning knowing Peeper was effortlessly moving in God's ultimate intention for her—and that made her glorious.

When it came time to move from our country home in Oklahoma to the California Coast, we donated Peeper to a college campus pond where she now swims with many beautiful swans—hope your doing fine, Peeper.

Our kids are easily inspired if we take time to be childlike and enter their imaginary world. Deep, profound truths can easily be deposited in these electric moments. **One such truth I urge you to instill is their God given responsibility to be stewards and governs of God's earth.**

"The heaven—even the heavens, are the Lord's but; the earth he hath
given (nathan) to the children of men."
PSALM 115:16 KJ

The Hebrew word **"Nathan,"** #5414 here does not mean to give away but is more accurately translated **"assigned" or given the responsibility of governing, stewarding or occupying as God's representative.** In other words, we are to re-present the Kingdom rule of the Lord Jesus Christ. We can't underestimate our child's inclination to thrive in this place of supremacy. They will amaze us with their instinctive ability to be God's manager here on earth. After all, did we ever have to teach them to be in charge or try to be the boss? No, it's innate but just has to be redirected.

I remember explaining this concept of stewarding God's earth to my young girls. I motivated them by their desire to be a "boss" over something. You know as a young person, they don't have much authority, they're always being told what to do. So I just asked them how, would they like to be the "boss?" Of course, this got their attention. I rattled on as to how they could be the "boss"—the "boss" of their own mind and body. Then, they had lots of laughs telling their bad attitude to go and that grumpy face to smile. It's etched in their DNA; they're programmed to be King of the Mountain. **We had great fun learning what it means to be a "boss."**

Marked for Glory

I remember a moment when my younger daughter, Grace embraced this novel idea. As a seven year old, she was the surrogate "mother" of a stray, black tomboy cat named Nesser. She strolled him tucked in her baby carriage donned in a bonnet. He even licked drops of milk squirted from his baby bottle. One day he turned up missing and broke his "mother's" heart. We searched high and low but there was no Nesser to be found. As the days passed our hope to ever find him waned.

One morning in prayer, Holy Spirit had a word for Grace, "You're the mean warring princess at the gates of hell—rise up and take your authority."

Something came over her and she began to stomp around the living room, commanding Nesser to return home. She rebuked the thief and released an angelic rescue. Miracle of miracles, suddenly we heard the floor furnace grate begin to rattle and a half-dead Nesser pushed his way up a heater vent right before our eyes. We grabbed the emaciated, bedraggled cat and sped to the vet. He was confounded and said this cat has been bitten by a rattle snake and shouldn't be alive. He obviously went down in the heater vent to die. The swelling was closing off his throat from breathing. Losing small animals to poisonous snake bites was common medical practice to this rural veterinarian.

"I'll treat him as best I can, but don't expect his comeback, I've never seen one make it yet."

Any way, you know the rest of the story. Nesser lived, defying all medical practice and testified in Grace's heart that surely she had "princely dominion" and dark, thieving spirits had to obey her voice. After all, Jesus her elder brother is the Son— the Prince of the King, Father God! That's why our prophetic kids must have everyday, heartfelt revelation of how Father God has disarmed principalities and triumphed over them in the cross. (Colossians 2:15) **Who they are in Christ's triumph must crystallize in their hearts.**

"For in Him dwells all the fullness of the Godhead bodily. And you are complete in Him, which is the head of all principality and power."
COLOSSIANS 2:9,10 KJ

Jesus is the apostle and high priest of our confession. He authorizes our **confession, "homologia"** which translates in Greek, #3671, **"to say the same thing God says."** When our kids say what they hear the Father saying, then their voices resound from heaven's governmental throne, displacing demonic ruling principalities and powers. **He only authorizes those things He breathes in intimacy as we meet Him in heavenly places.**

"Wherefore, holy brethren, partakers of the
heavenly calling, consider the Apostle and High
Priest of our **confession (homologia)**, Christ Jesus."
HEBREWS 3:1 PARAPHRASED

As our kids visualize themselves in heavenly
places, their throne room prayers are always heard.

"If my people, which are called by my name,
shall humble themselves, and pray,
and seek my face, and turn from their wicked ways;
Then will I hear from Heaven,
and will forgive their sin, and will heal their land."
2 CHRONICLES 7:14 KJ

**Where will He hear from?   He will hear the
prayers being prayed from heaven—prayed in this
place—in His throne room by those who access His
Presence.**   Oh doesn't He say, we're seated in
heavenly places?   Oh, that's why Revelation 4:1
invites us to "come up."

**"Then I looked, and oh!—a door open into
Heaven. The trumpet-voice— called out. 'Ascend
and enter. I'll show you what happens next'"**
REVELATION 4:1 THE MESSAGE

Immutable Promise

I am a living answer to one of those prayers,
prayed in His throne room that took 150 years
before it thrived. I've even heard of 1,000 year old
seeds found in Egyptian tombs being planted and
life springing forth. Imagine that even some of

Jesus' prayers are yet to come to pass. But trust me, surely we will descend out of heaven like a bride all beautified and adorned for our husband. He's seeking those He can show Himself strong in their behalf.

"God is always on the alert,
constantly on the lookout for people
who are totally committed to him."
2 CHRONICLES 16:9 THE MESSAGE

There will be an end time generation, testifying of God's answered prayers—prayed in that place— that heavenly place. There are millenniums of compounding prayers about to spill over the bowls in heaven—ready to tip and release His glory. These are the synergistic prayers of His saints about ready to hit planet earth.

"The smoke of the incense, together with the
prayers of the saints, went up before God from the
angel's hand. Then the angel took the censer,
filled it with fire from the altar,
and hurled it on the earth;
and there came peals of thunder,
rumblings, flashes of lightning and an earthquake."
REVELATION 8:4,5 NIV

Surely we are poised for the "greatest show on earth—don't miss it!"

Listen to just one story of a promise fulfilled in my lifetime—a prayer stored in those heavenly bowls not over flowing until three generations later.

My great-great-great grandfather, Orceneth Fisher was an early apostle inspired by the zeal of

God to spread holiness on the mission fields of the Pacific Coast in the 1850's. One article documented Orcenth's sermon in the debauched drunken sailor port of San Francisco. Satan had this gold rush town of lawless, motley outlaws in his grip. This preacher of holiness, mantled with the tangible glory rocked California's foreboding atmosphere. Here is a first hand account of one of his meetings.

"It seemed as if we could almost hear the hush
of Pentecostal wind and see the tongues of flame.
The very house seemed to be rocking on its
foundations. I had seen and heard preachers
who glowed in the pulpit… this man burned.
His words poured forth in a molten flood,
his face shone like a furnace heated within,
his large blue eyes flashed with the lightning
of impassioned sentiment that no heart could resist.
All seemed to feel the mighty blast
of God's blowing breath
as this man was transfigured before us."
"A FOUNDATION IS LAID" BY SOPHIA SCHLOEMAN

His prophetic journals are in my keeping and like hot stones they lay as embers on my heart. I am haunted by his great sacrifice and the generational transfer that begs my passionate completion.

"As I (Orceneth) write this jostling on horseback through the deep snow my fingers are almost too stiff to write. The traveling is heavy but we must make it to the military post by night, or else… "

What was in these treasured journals whose writings he risked his life for—a destiny matrix for those who would follow. He had to document this indwelling glory he carried— inspiring us to contend for the same manifestation of the sons of God. **You know Jesus came as a holy advertisement of what a mere man consumed with Holy Spirit would look like. Jesus' fame has gone abroad and calls to those marked to carry His glory.**

God is a God of the generations. It takes an Abraham, Isaac and Jacob, the three fold cord, to secure the promises on the Father's heart. This prophetic word from Orceneth's journal released an inheritance into my grasping soul. He penned this ageless prayer with frozen fingers while riding horseback through treacherous Indian land. Three generations passed as his prayer lay silent in the hardened heart of his progeny. Yet one day, the heavens opened and a mighty rush of his impetuous zeal consumed me. Prayers prayed in that place are forever alive—they never die!

"Be careful, Daughter, of the rearing of your sons and daughters. The fires that burn within me will me their heritage. Surely, an abundant life of opportunities for service awaits them in the future."

As I read these ageless words from his journal— they bolted through my being as shafts of light—I knew they were alive, still burning with destiny before the embers of His throne.

Orcenth's prophetic eyes scanned far into future generations beyond the tragic pioneering era that his own daughter Mary lived. She had lost 4 of his 5 grand daughters to the deprivation of the civil war years as the only food available was cornmeal mush or biscuits crumbled in milk and coffee. On a rampage in the Texas frontier, Comanche Indians had circled her cabin throwing a crazed skunk impaled on a forked stick through her cabin window. Mary huddled with her children in the dark night smothered with skunk odor and the curdling war cries of fierce raiding Indians. Lighting a candle, she found the skunk burrowed in Dora Jane's cradle. Mary nursed her pierced and bleeding-bitten fingers with turpentine and tallow, only to lose her to death's grip. How deep the grief as Mary felt Dora Jane's tiny form stiffen in her arms—convulsion after convulsion.

Oh, so costly the price to lay an apostolic foundation. We must inspire our children with the heroic trail of sacrifice—sacrifice that blazes our privileged, blessed life with the immutable promises guaranteed from prayers prayed in that place—heaven's throne.

As our prophetic kids realize they are truly princes—off springs of the Highest King, they will rule in "princely dominion" as the great cloud of witnesses cheers them on from heaven's window sill.

"Not one of these people (heroes of faith),
even though their lives of faith were exemplary,
got their hands on what was promised. God had a
better plan for us, that their faith would come
together to make one completed whole, their lives
of faith not complete apart from ours."
Hebrews 11:39 The Message

As we grab the baton to cross the finish line of His Kingdom race, know we're carried on the shoulders of apostles and prophets of old. You know they always assign the fastest runner for the last lap of the relay race. Our prophetic kids might be that chosen runner. We must infuse them with a quantum leap surge for this last lap. They must be strong and courageous so the mystery hidden from the ages will be revealed—the clandestine promise realized in them.

> "...the glorious riches of this mystery, which is
> Christ in you, the hope of glory."
> *COLOSSIANS 1:27 THE MESSAGE*

CHAPTER NINE

GOD IS IN THIS PLACE

Eyes Wide-Open Life

Jacob had a destiny dream that set the course of his life.

> "And he dreamed, and behold a ladder set up on
> the earth and the top of it reached to heaven and
> behold the angels of God ascending and descending
> on it. And behold the Lord stood above it and said,
> I am the Lord God of Abraham,
> thy father, and the God of Isaac: and in thy seed
> shall all the families of the earth be blessed…
> for I will not leave thee, until
> I have done that which I have spoken to thee of."
> *GENESIS 28:12,13-15 NKJ*

Jacob had a profound response when he saw the heavenly staircase and heard God's voice at the top.

"God is in this place…truly." And I didn't even know it!… He whispered in awe, 'Incredible… Wonderful… Holy. This is God's House. This is the Gate of Heaven.'"

GENESIS 28:16,17 THE MESSAGE

Our kids have to have their own "eureka" moments. Foundational to their destiny is the revelation that they themselves are a literal "gate" that can flood Heaven's atmosphere into the earth. They are a virtual portal, an open door that funnels God's glory and establishes His Kingdom on earth as it is in heaven.

How does this happen? It happens in a "face to face," moment by moment, awareness of Holy Spirit's Presence. It's then they realize that, "God is in this place"! What place? God is in the place of their Spirit man—their Holy of Holies. In this place, reverence for His presence safeguards their every thought and action. In this place, the "rhema" Word—the God breathed Word, exhales — breathing life into their very being.

Ironically, when God appeared to Jacob, He didn't mention Jacob's desperation of being a fugitive on the run in a death defying desert, but only promised, "I am in this place."

God didn't stoke a pity party with Jacob saying, "Wow, you poor boy with only a rock for a pillow and that nasty brother of yours, hunting you down like a wild animal." God overlooked Jacob's momentary problems and spoke prophetically of his divine destiny. This prophetic vision was so enlivening that Jacob's troubles paled in the revelation of his glorious call from God.

So it is with us, our revelation of the Lord's presence and guarantee of His covenant blessings will guarantee a glorious journey and shield us from the hardships of life. Jacob's visionary encounter empowered him to take his hard rock of a pillow, anoint it with oil and build a sacred altar of worship. **God encounters allow us to live an amazing, "eyes wide-open life" under His sunrise smile! Let's cultivate divine encounters with our kids!**

"Jacob was up first thing in the morning. He took the stone he had used for his pillow and stood it up as a memorial pillar and poured oil over it. He christened the place Bethel (God's House).
GENESIS 28:18 THE MESSAGE

We see here how Jacob took the hard stones life had dealt him and with those same stones, built an altar of worship. **Notice this is when the anointing oil began to flow in his life.**

Abraham also worshiped God in the middle of his greatest test. Even when the Lord seemingly asked him to sacrifice his long awaited, promised son Isaac, Abraham showed his unrelenting trust in Papa God's goodness. We must teach our kids to never withhold anything that God might ask of them. What ever the situation demands, Jesus is just setting them up for Kingdom greatness and a lavish inheritance.

> "... take now your son, your only son Isaac,
> whom you love... and offer him there ... "
> GENESIS 22:2 AMPLIFIED

Notice how Abraham responded to the seeming death of his life time destiny dream, Isaac. He knew the Lord well enough not to insult His divine intentions—for His God was a God of Life.

> "... I (Abraham) and the young man (Isaac)
> will go yonder and worship and come again to you."
> GENESIS 22: 5 AMPLIFIED

Life holds immense challenges, so in order that our kids not stumble along the way in bitter discouragement, we must insulate them with a worshiper's heart such as Abraham and Isaac had.

Isaac felt the heavy wood press his shoulders as they toted the knife and fire pot up the rugged hill of Mount Moriah. Where was the lamb, Isaac wondered? As a young boy, he had often offered sacrifices with his father many times, yet this time something was different. As Isaac felt the tug of cords binding him on the altar, he surrendered completely. In total obedience, he lay abandoned to his father's will. As Abraham stretched forth his hand and took the knife to slay his son—even then Isaac lay still. What if Isaac had struggled, resisting his fathers bidding? Maybe in the confusion Abraham might have missed the Lord's voice.

> "And the angel of the Lord called to him from
> heaven and said, Abraham. Abraham!
> He answered. Here I am.

And He said, Do not lay your hand on the lad."

Then they named the place, "The Lord Will Provide"—realizing they were covenant partners with Jehovah Jireh, the One that "sees" from afar off and has already provided. In Isaac's most tragic moment, his dad was right there imparting a rich legacy of Truth.

"Abraham prophetically said, my son,
God Himself will provide a lamb..."

The literal Hebrew translation states, "**God will provide Himself a lamb**"—not, "God Himself will provide." A subtle difference, but this understanding will bring immeasurable peace. Father God locks His bountiful supply within Himself—so lavish that He guards it within Himself!

Jesus doesn't just bring healing—He is Jehovah Rapha, our healer, resident on the inside. He, Himself, is our secured health, prosperity, victory, etc and can not be separated from His promises. **He Himself is the promise. He is the provision and does not bring something from outside of Himself. These covenant blessings are really Him, tucked away in our heart of hearts. Jesus doesn't just provide a lamb—He is the sacrificial Lamb of Calvary. In Him is embedded every good thing!**

Jesus does it all... all by Himself... if we just worship Him. The greatest glory that will ever happen to us has already happened—Jesus exploding big on the inside of us. In the midst of trial, we can impart incredible truths to our kids only realized through experience.

Abraham was saying, "No worries, Son," this God we worship is not indifferent or distant, but every tear shed is saved in His bottle of remembrance. Nothing will be lost—if we just worship Him. I love this acronym for "F.E.A.R." "F," is for false; "E," for evidence; "A," for appearing and "R," for real. "FALSE EVIDENCE APPEARING AS REAL"! As we adore our loving Father all fear has to leave.

He gathers every scrap of hardship — transforming it for His glory. He hides blessings in Himself as something given outside of Himself could be intercepted or corrupted. He, Himself, is in this place—the place of worship.

Eyes of the Heart

I remember when Abby asked me, "Why is God invisible? I hear His voice Grandma, but why can't I see Him?"

I could tell she was perplexed and somewhat annoyed at this unseen realm presented to her young heart. How could someone that loved her so much hide in obscurity and be invisible? After all, her small world was so sensory. Her delight was snuggling in bed between piles of her squishy animal friends. Night time, you'd find her buried beneath mounds of floppy-eared, furry paws all cuddled in her arms. She was a very, feely, touchy child. Her little heart was longing to see and touch this invisible God that she so loved.

Wow, this was quite a question! In simple, childlike language I began to explain how she has two sets of eyes—one, her natural set of eye balls for seeing physical things and then the eyes of her heart for seeing things hidden in the Spirit realm. The apostle Paul wrote of this.

> "I pray that the eyes of your heart
> may be enlightened..."
> *EPHESIANS 1:18 NIV*

The eyes of our children's heart are easily enlightened—they like to keep it simple. Their "Heaven Friend" is not religious or preachy. Becoming like little children pleases God when we play in their imaginary world.

I remember one magical night when Abby and I lay out under the stars snuggled in our blanket. We were so in awe of the beauty of His creation.

She said, Grandma, "let's spend the night here... could we... could we? He's here... He's here... I can feel Him." She lifted her sweet voice and it floated into the vast diamond studded sky. She began to sing "Twinkle, Twinkle Little Star" as only a two year old can. The atmosphere was pristine and we shifted into heavenly places. Oh, what a treasured night when we sang out under the stars cuddled in His love.

In such times, He indelibly imprints His great love in our kid's heart of hearts. Familiarize them with the stories of Abraham, Daniel, Ezekiel, Stephen and others that saw the Lord as clearly as an earthly friend. **Inspire them, that they too can see the Lord with the eyes of their heart. Prepare them to expect a suddenly, even at the most unlikely times as these great patriarchs did.**

"The Lord appeared to Abraham near the great
trees of Mamre while he was sitting at the
entrance to his tent in the heat of the day."
GENESIS 18:1 NIV

"As I (Daniel) looked, thrones were set in place,
and the Ancient of Days took his seat.
His clothing was as white as snow;
the hair of his head was white like wool.
His throne was flaming with fire,
and its wheels were all ablaze.
**A river of fire was flowing,
coming out from before him… "**
DANIEL 7:9,10 NIV

"Above the dome there was something that looked
like a throne, sky-blue like a sapphire, with a
humanlike figure towering above the throne.
From what I (Ezekiel) could see, from the waist up
he looked like burnished bronze and from the waist
down like a blazing fire. Brightness everywhere!
The way a rainbow springs out of the sky on a rainy
day-that's what is was like.
It turned out to be the Glory of God!"
EZEKIEL 1:26-28 THE MESSAGE

"But **Stephen,** full of the Holy Spirit, looked up to
heaven and **saw the glory of God, and Jesus
standing at the right hand of God.**

Look, he said, I see heaven open and the son of
Man standing at the right hand of God."

"… Jesus came and stood among them and said,
'Peace be with you!' After he said this, he showed
them his hands and side. **The disciples were
overjoyed when they saw the Lord.**"
JOHN 20:19-20 NIV

"God-you're my God! I can't get enough of you!
So here I am in the place of worship,
**eyes open to see you in the sanctuary
and behold your power and glory.**"
PSALM 63:1,2 PARAPHRASED

Oh what a beautiful thing to worship God with
your children and expect an epiphany—when the
concealed is disclosed and His grace envisions us to
really see. It's often in the most common, ordinary
times that His ecstasy grabs us unexpectedly. I
remember when my Amy as a toddler stood eye ball
to eye ball with the fresh bloom of a lilac Iris.

With all the dramatics of a toddler, she sighed,
"Momma, this thrills my heart." **There was a divine
infusion that ordinary morning—God loves it when
we take time with our kids to see with the eyes of
our heart.**

Remember when Moses experienced the bush
that set on fire. This was a common occurrence in
the sweltering desert to see bushes burn. But this
bush wasn't consumed—something caught his eye.
What if Moses had been "ho hum," after all he'd
been around this mountain for 40 years and nothing
had ever happened before. But something urged
him to step aside and look. Maybe the Lord had

been waiting for him to expect a suddenly and see with his prophetic, "seer" eyes—all along.

"When the Lord saw that he turned aside to see, God called to him out of the midst of the bush and said, Moses, Moses! And he said, Here am I… and God said the place on which you stand is holy ground."
EXODUS 3:2,4,5 AMPLIFIED

When my girls were growing up, we were always looking for a glimpse of Him in our prayer times. Before they could write, they would draw what the eyes of their heart had seen. Journaling is a great way to stretch their "seer," visionary prophetic anointing and honor His visitation, even if it's just chalk on the drive way.

We talked about what it felt like to be close to Him and did He whisper any thing? We stomped around the back yard hunting for fragrances. But it was only when our faces sniffed the Honey Suckle up close that we swooned in the perfume. Oh, the pleasures of being close to Him. Then, we would relax under a tall tree, resting in His presence.

It was so amazing, by the time they were seven or eight they both had had open destiny visions that shaped their future callings. My daughter, Grace, saw her music notes on a key board encircling the globe. Today she is an ordained psalmist that ministers healing and deliverance under an open heaven to the nations. My other daughter, Amy saw her feet dancing in swirls of blessing as she walked the earth in authority. Today she is operating in an apostolic anointing with her husband, Scott, as ministers of a revival center.

When their daughter Abby was just two years old, she announced to her Dad at bedtime prayers, that an angel had come to her and said they were going to have a baby boy. They were shocked as it was not in their plans but her spirit heard clearly and it came to pass just as the angel had told her. **We can't underestimate our children. After all, their Spirits are just as big as our Spirit. As we sensitize them to the realm of the supernatural, true living really begins.**

Stairway to Heaven

Following are copies from my daughters, *"Prayer, the Holy Punch" Journal for Kids*. Please feel free to duplicate it as a template for intimacy. We have had tremendous testimonies of kids being activated to experience the supernatural wonders of Heaven. This is available on our web site along with other Prophetic Kids Resources.

Oh life is so sweet as we long for His presence, "for one day in His courts is better than a thousand any where." **The absolute best part of life is being child like and experiencing God with our kids!**

PRAYER

the HOLY PUNCH

☆☆☆☆☆☆☆☆☆☆☆☆☆☆☆☆☆☆☆☆☆☆☆☆☆☆☆☆☆☆☆☆☆☆☆☆☆☆☆

<u>Name:</u>

<u>Week of:</u>

MEMORY VERSE ✍✍✍✍✍✍✍✍✍✍✍✍✍

TIME SPENT WITH GOD ⇑⇑⇑⇑⇑⇑⇑⇑⇑⇑⇑⇑⇑⇑

Mon.	Tues.	Wed.	Thur.	Fri.	Sat.	Sun.
☐	☐	☐	☐	☐	☐	☐

WHAt GOD tOLD Me tHi2 WeeK:

○dreams ○words ○visions ○scriptures ○revelations

Heaven's curtain is poised to open, revealing the wildest, most spectacular display of God's beauty. We live in a high-tech visual generation and if we abandon our kids to Sunday school historic Bible stories, statistics tell us over 70% will leave the church and never return. They will be inoculated against exuding His vibrant glory and lulled into being a passive spectator as real life passes them by. **We can't let our little prophets miss the greatest show on earth—the face—the face of Jesus!**

"And me? I plan on looking you full in the face. When I get up, I'll see your full stature and live heaven on earth."
PSALM 17:15 THE MESSAGE

As we prepare our kids for dual citizenship, they will ascend and descend between heaven and earth welcome to throne room business.

They will be privy to His Kingdom plans and return to execute His will on earth—extraterrestrial "Scottys" where they say, "beam up me up as You will Lord." Let's raise little Jacobs that encounter Jesus, the Ladder.

"And he dreamed (Jacob): a stairway was set on the ground and it reached all the way to the sky; angels of God were going up and going down on it. Then God was right before him, saying, I am God, the God of Abraham your father… and all people of the earth will be blessed through you and your offspring."
GENESIS 28:12,13 THE MESSAGE

Let's set our kids on heaven's staircase, releasing them as envoys between heaven and earth!

CHAPTER TEN

———— ∞ ————

BIG PRAYERS FROM LITTLE PEOPLE

Culture Shock

———— ∞ ————

There are difficult times ahead and the best counter attack is the raising up of a prophetic generation of young people who have prophetic eyes to see as God sees. God sees His son, Jesus and His anointed kids triumphing over evil.

> "What fools the nations are to rage against the
> Lord!... But God in heaven merely laughs!
> He is amused by all their puny plans."
> *PSALM 2:4-6 LIVING BIBLE*

Scripture forewarns us of the cultural climate brooding in the end times.

"As the end approaches, people are going to be
self-absorbed, money hungry, self-promoting,
stuck-up, profane, contemptuous of parents,
crude, coarse, dog-eat-dog, unbending, slanderers,
impulsively wild, savage, cynical, treacherous,
ruthless, bloated windbags, addicted to lust, and
allergic to God. They'll make a show of religion,
but behind the scenes they're animals.

2 TIMOTHY 3:1-5 THE MESSAGE

We no longer live in a "Leave it to Beaver"
world. That story book life style of the Cleaver's
gathered around Mom's home cooking discussing
Wally having shot a "spit wad" at school—is
history! Beaver's mom, June, has taken off her
apron and working two jobs, while Beaver's dad,
Ward, has spied the "gay" next door.

What worked for kids in the 50's isn't enough
for today's pressing culture. In fact, we are in the
midst of a "culture shock." Let's face it, many
moms are stressed out, self-absorbed and dad is
solacing himself at the "stiletto-heeled " happy
hour. What used to work is not working any more.
Regular youth group attendance and the, "now I lay
me down to sleep" night time prayers are helpless
before our perverted culture. Like it or not, our
kids are thrust into this malaise of "culture shock."
Let's help them not bite the dust of a sickened anti-
Christ system.

"Arise, cry out in the night: in the beginning
of the watches **pour out your heart like water
before the face of the Lord:**

lift up your hands toward Him
for the life of your young children,
that faint for hunger in the top of every street."
LAMENTATIONS 2:19 KJ

Our kids are starving for God's power and glory—they faint for hunger roaming the malls—zoned out in voyeuristic cyber space. All of His power is hidden and must be searched for in His presence! Our "churched kids" are famished from having been presented a cold, distant God like an unfamiliar absentee father they've never known or touched.

"And His brightness (Jesus) was like the sunlight;
rays streamed from His hand,
and **there [in the sunlike splendor]**
was the hiding place of His power.
HABAKKUK 3:4 AMPLIFIED

Our kids must experience His glorious presence—the hiding place of His power.

I remember my girls telling me as teen agers, "... you know Mom, if all we had was our youth groups, we would have never stuck with Jesus."

No matter how great our church is, they can't saturate them with enough piercing devotion for His heart—this He reserves for Mom and Dad.

The following pages are exact, word for word, copies of misspelled, scribblings—penned from kid's hearts. Often when I open my stored boxes of these hand-written prayer requests, I fall on my face asking for a new breed of parents that delve into the inner recesses of their children—touching their deep needs that can't be verbalized.

May it motivate us to be ready for that moment when we will stand face to face with the Lord and hear Him say, "Well done, my faithful one" or will we just hear, "Well?"

Candle in the Darkness—Can Anyone See Me?

For a season my daughters and I were children's ministers in our "rock'n, full gospel" church. Our celebrity pastor even had a television ministry and body guards but we had to bring our own pencil supply for the kids to even write these prayer requests. Surely the lamp stand was going out in the Temple but we just didn't see it. We must be so careful whose spiritual authority we come under—for the anointing transfers, clean or unclean—"like Pastor—like sheep." His spiritual covering can bless or contaminate.

Up to this time, we assumed most parents were doing a pretty decent job of raising their kids… after all they were Christians and their kids were in Children's Church. But we were in for a shock. Every week we asked the kids for their prayer requests and I guess their little hearts say it all. At first we were perplexed… what's going on here? Then month after month, I held hundreds of these, "Big Prayers From Little People" before the Lord, crying out for His mercy. Deep grief swept over me as I treasured these snippets of their heartfelt emotions. Sense their pain with me as "church kids" flounder in the haze of neglect.

"Stop the Bad Stuff in My Home"

"I feel lonely, I feel scared, Pastor."

"Jesus, please bless my mom so she can wake up
and be a good mom."

"Please God, don't let no bad happen."

"I want love."

"Everyone calls me fatty, I need you to help me."

"Let me be happy all my life."

"Guide my mom into the light
and not be a lesbiand."

"My sister and I fight, I pray we can stop."

"No botty likes me, I am sad."

"To help me."

"Make stuff better."

"Stop the bad stuff in my home."

"That my school, starts to worship God."

"People don't like me because I look ugly."

"Dear Lord, bless my becuss
I have not got my bless yet."

"Everyday I pray so I wont have a bad dream."

"I want to be good."

I need prayer on me."

"More want to read my Bible."

"Help my brother be nice to me."

"Pray for my mom, she is always yelling at me
and so is my grandma."

"I need wheels on my roller blades."

"God, I need the tire of my bike pumped."

"God, help me learn to ride a bike."

Have times gotten so bad that children have to ask God to help them learn to ride their bike or pump a forgotten tire? What ever happened to the "Kodak camera times" when families captured Dad helping Junior mount his bike? And what about magical bed time talks, when drossy kids shared the deep secrets of their hearts and pain melted like wax under Mom's soothing touch?

"I Need My Dad"

"Help…my father put a gun to my head,
pray he'll get off drugs."

"I'm very sad because he gets drunk and yells."

"I want to see my dad again that

I haven't saw for two years."

"I need my dad."

"I don't have any money
but I've been wanting a dad."

"I pray that my father comes back
because I cry for him sometime."

"I need my family to have fun together
and eat dinner together"

"Pray that my dad will not yell at me
and my sister anymore."

"I need peece in my family. For my dad to kom hom
so that I kan sae I luv him."

"I need hope in my family."

"My mom to come to my birthday party."

"Please, I need help
my mom is fighting with my dad."

"My dad to come and visit more often,
he can't come see us
because he don't want to cry in front of us."

"Help."

"Help," this request says it all! This young one can't even articulate the tangled maze inside. In his tender heart, he can't begin to sort out where all the hurt is from or how it could ever go away. I wonder what the heart of God feels as the serpent slithers through the virgin soil of His youth? Think about it, these prayer requests are from "churched kids" caught in the malaise of a sickened culture. They are helpless hunted ones, stalked by the ancient foe to torment the heart of God through that which God loves the most, His kids.

"Rip the Disvoice Head Off"

"I hope my family don't get a devourse."

"I feel lonely without my dad."

"My mom and dad got diverce,
pray that I can get through with it."

"God can you help my mom and dad
stop getting a devorce?"

"I hope my family don't get a disvoice."

"I need my dad."

"I wanna know where my dad is."

"I want prayer on my dad plese."

"For my dad to come see me."

"See my dad morr."

"I need my dad to get saved and stop drink."

"Pray for my mom and dad to be friends."

"My family needs love."

"For the Lord to have mercy on my dad."

"Mom and dad are getting a devorce,
the're yelling at each other."

"I'm sad because my dad drinks."

"Please pray for me that my dad will talk to me,
because my mother has a boy friend
and he blames it on me."

"My dad needs help."

"Can you help me and my daddy?"

"Pray for me to get a dad."

"Dad!"

"I want to have a good Christian dad."

"I pray my mom and dad stop fiting."

**"I need my mom to come back,
if she can't, tell her that I love her."**

"I pray the devil will leave my family alone."

How many ways can you spell divorce? Devorse... divos... davors... devourse... diverce... devorce... disvoice. Kids might not know how to spell the word "divorce" but their hearts know well its devastation. This one prayer request says it all!

"Please God, help my family not get a devorse."

To this child, divorce isn't just between Mom and Dad but a gouge piercing his soul—one dream lopped off and then another and another. The razor cuts deep as he shuffles to gather the **scattered pieces.** It's only then that the prophetic edge of God's Word can stop the carnage. It's then that single parents and blended families must even more so, "lay their young upon the altars of the Lord" and like Abraham, "go yonder with their kids and worship" Our blossoming prophets must live out of their heavenly identity—enthroned with their royal family and myriad of angels.

God is passionate for having sons and daughters—kids who bear His glorious image. His original intention has never changed since the Garden of Eden. That's why Satan has so ravaged fatherhood in order to disfigure the earthly reflection of Himself.

The "nabiy" prophet was anointed to see into the Spirit realm—these "seer" prophets only spoke out of what they had seen in the Spirit. Like Jesus, they only did what they saw the Father doing

David the Prophet, knew prophetically that His Father would have the final say about His kids.

"God Himself will be a father to the fatherless...
He gives families to the lonely."
PSALM 68:5,6 LIVING BIBLE

"Although my father and my mother have
forsaken me, yet the Lord will take me up
[adopt me as His child]."
PSALM 27:10 AMPLIFIED

"We Don't Have No Dollars"

I don't know about you but I had never heard of the word "debt" when I was seven years old. Hundreds of pre-teen prayers strain under the financial pressure in their homes. Their tender shoulders are not meant to carry the curse of poverty.

"I am having finachle problems."

"My mommy and me need money."

"Some money so we can get food."

"I would like to have more money that I have now."

"We don't have no dollars."
"Some more muney."

"Need money."

"That my families financial problems stop."

"My mom has financial problems,
she is single and is struggling."

"My mom got a new job and I got love now."

"We are in debt."

There is a pattern here. The child sees his family's financial need as his own deficiency. Somehow, he feels responsible for something he can do nothing about. He's caught in the maze of debt, crying out for help. Kids internalize lack as a reflection of themselves—worthless and not enough.

Riches in Glory

I still remember my stinging tears as they splashed on stacks of our unpaid bills. But I learned to rejoice at my girls "garage sell" Easter dresses as I sewed lace on the collars and ribboned sashes to beautify their girly image. They never felt the sting of poverty as I shielded their tender hearts, always making them feel precious and valuable… insuring them of the Lord's faithful provision. It was then I began to shout in the face of lack and declare:

"You've never seen the righteous forsaken
or their seed begging bread."
PSALM 37:25 KJ

"...for it is God that gives you power to get wealth,
that He may establish His covenant..."
DEUTERONOMY 8:18 KJ

Children are our inheritance from God,
something He entrusts to us as a temporary gift to
guard and protect and then return in beauty and
dignity. God is not a stingy taskmaster. He will
repay our diligence as we grab hold of our priestly
anointing and position our kids before His holy
face.

**"See that you do not look down
on one of these little ones.
For I tell you that their angels in heaven
always see the face of my Father in heaven."**
MATTHEW 18:10 NIV

"And whoever welcomes a little child like this in
my name, welcomes me. But if anyone, causes one
of these little ones who believe in me to sin,
it would be better for him to have a large millstone
hung around his neck
and to be drowned in the depths of the sea."
MATTHEW 18:6 NIV

There is a great transfer of wealth coming for
those who have eyes to see it. We must raise this
extraterrestrial generation to live outside the limits
of earth and tap into heaven's economy for their
source of blessing. All other institutions and
traditional means of supply are languishing under
the present anti-Christ system intended to choke
the flow of resources to the nations.

"And there was a **famine in the land**... and Isaac
sowed seed in that land and **received in the same**

year a hundred times as much as he had planted,
and the Lord favored him with blessings.
And Isaac became great and gained more and more
until he became very wealthy and distinguished. He
owned flocks, herds and a great supply of servants,
and the Philistines envied him."
GENESIS 26:1; 12-14 AMPLIFIED

"Praise the Lord! For all who fear God and trust in
Him are blessed beyond expression. Yes, happy is
the man who delights in doing his commands.
His children shall be honored everywhere,
for good men's sons have a special heritage.
"He himself shall be wealthy,
and his good deeds will never be forgotten."
PSALMS 112:1-3 LIVING BIBLE

"We went through fire and flood. But in the end,
You brought us into wealth and great abundance."
PSALMS 66:12 LIVING BIBLE

"My God shall supply all your need according to
His riches in **glory ("doxa")** by Christ Jesus."
PHILIPPIANS 4:19 KJ

The Greek word used here for **"glory"** is **"doxa,"**
#1391. **"Doxa"** means an image or appearance that
catches the eye or attracts attention, commanding
recognition. It speaks of splendor, brilliance and
perfections of God's divine nature. If our kids are
to survive the tumultuous financial storm
approaching, then they must be plugged into the
economy of heaven. Their eyes must be fastened on
the Lord's glorious countenance. Only God's divine
favor on their lives will insure safety and provision
in the upcoming upheaval.

Where does God store the vault of His riches—in His glorious presence! All of His power and anointing is hidden in Christ. All of our kid's expectations for promotion, favor and honor must rest upon the One who alone exalts and gives them the power to get wealth. God Himself will give them witty ideas and inventions insuring they are "earth blessers."

The days of a college degree bringing job security is over! Time-honored US icon corporations are over leveraged and collapsing under the vice of greed and misdealings. Long standing institutions are cratering under deceptive, altered accounting practices that have fed their lust for undue profit. Money markets and IRA retirement savings are vaporizing as we speak. We, as the tutor of this prophetic generation must shift our kids into the "glorious riches in Christ Jesus"—seek His Kingdom and all other things will be added to them!

CHAPTER ELEVEN

─────── ∞ ───────

ℳistaken Identity

Lifting the Veil

─────── ∞ ───────

𝒯he Apostle John was on the Isle of Patmos, when the Heaven's opened and a man approached announcing the marriage feast. This fellow servant so much expressed Jesus, so testified and gave evidence of Him and His anointing so powerful that **John actually mistook Him for Jesus and started to worship him.** The visitor had to restrain him saying:

> "Refrain! You must not do that! I am only
> another servant with you and your brethren
> who <u>have (echo)</u> the witness of Jesus:
> worship God:
> for the testimony of Jesus is the spirit of prophecy."
> *REVELATION 19:10 PARAPHRASED*

The word "**have**" is "**echo**" in Greek and implies the special relationship between a husband and his wife. In other words, only the bride can become one flesh with her groom and testify, giving evidence of her glorious groom. We see right from the beginning in Genesis 2:24 that husband and wife are of the same flesh and bone … "**they shall become one flesh.**"

The heavenly messenger that John saw was a "billboard," so to speak—an advertisement of what the Fire Bride would look like as we approach the wedding feast. The very title of the book of Revelation is "**apokalupsis,**" meaning to, "take the cover off or unveil." I believe John had a glimpse of the glory unveiled in the end-time saints.

Yes, we can be like Mary at the wedding in Cana when she pulled the future into the present as her faith prompted Jesus to do His first miracle of turning water into wine. Hadn't Jesus said that it was not yet His time? (John 2:4) Nevertheless, her prophetic insight into His future destiny, prompted Him to step out of today into tomorrow.

This changing of water into wine is a prophetic picture of the glorification of His saints. We might think our time is not yet, but Jesus is urging us to step into our destiny now! In this outpouring of the latter rain, we will be looking more like saints coming down from heaven, than ones on our way to heaven.

Jesus enlightened Lazarus' sister, Martha, with revelation of the "Now God…the Great I Am God…the faith is now God." I remember when Hebrews 11:1 became life to me and the, "faith is now," revelation unlocked promises that had been on hold for too long. My delayed promises flooded in as I stopped waiting around. **My "now faith," my "faith is now truth," is extravagantly flourishing in His present Truth.**

> "**Now faith is** the substance of things hoped for the evidence of things not seen."
> *HEBREWS 11:1 KJ*

> "Martha said, Master if you'd been here, my brother wouldn't have died...Jesus said, 'Your brother will be raised up.'" Martha replied, "I know that he will be raised up in the resurrection at the end of time." **"You don't have to wait for the End. I am, right now, Resurrection and Life."**
> *JOHN 11:21-25 THE MESSAGE*

You know the shortest verse in the Bible, "Jesus wept," happens at the grave side of Lazarus. What was Jesus weeping about? His grief wasn't for the loss of his friend Lazarus or the stench of death that entombed him. The real grief was that His followers misread Him as the God of the future and not the, "I am" of the present. Jesus wept that the bystanders were blind to His resurrection power. Their shortsighted memory now turned His very miracles against Him. They mocked His crocodile tears, implying He was a phony.

> "(bystanders)... Well, if he loved him so much, why didn't he do something to keep him from dying? After all he opened the eyes of a blind man."
> *JOHN 11:37 THE MESSAGE*

Jesus is eager to unveil His kingdom to anyone who has a heart to see—reveal it to anyone who would believe.

"The kingdom of God doesn't come by counting the days on the calendar. Nor when someone says, 'Look here! or 'There it is!' And why? Because God's kingdom is already among you.'"
LUKE 17:21 THE MESSAGE

There's a man listed in the Heroes of faith, Enoch. They say, he had a testimony that pleased God—a faith that pleased God.

"By faith Enoch was translated
that he should not see death; and was not found,
because God had translated him:
for before his translation he had
this **testimony (martureo)**, that he pleased God."
HEBREWS 11:5 KJ

This Greek word, **"martureo,"** #3140 translated **"testimony,"** tells us that Enoch so much gave evidence of Jesus—so much gave testimony of Him that God took him. Another form, **"marturia,"** #3141 is used in Hebrews 19:10 for, **"the testimony (marturia) of Jesus is the spirit of prophecy,"** that we discussed earlier.

"And Enoch walked with God:
and he was not; for God **took, (laqach)** him."
GENESIS 5:24 KJV

The Hebrew word, "laqach," #3947 can translate, "mingle." **Enoch so walked with God that he actually became one with God as they mingled together.** No—make no mistake about it, we are not divinity, yet scripture tells us to become "partakers of His divine nature." Quite a distinction—but oh so close!

> "According as his divine power **hath given**
> **unto us all things that pertain unto life**
> **and godliness,** through the knowledge of him
> that hath called us to glory and virtue.
> Whereby are given unto us exceeding great and
> precious promises that by these ye might be
> **partakers of the divine nature** having escaped the
> corruption that is in the world through lust."
> *2 PETER 1:3,4 KJV*

"Partake" means to participate. We do not possess His divinity, yet in His graciousness, He invites us to participate and share in His divinity. As a loving Father, He includes us, asking for our vote and voice in this heavenly partnership. Wow! He gives us all things that we need to become like God—His empowerment to "be like God."

May our kids catch this revelation concerning the available transformation. **We can't let our kids miss the greatest show on earth! Cry out with me that we not delay any promise that He wants to fulfill in our lifetime.**

> "The Government of Death, its constitution
> chiseled on stone tablets, had a dazzling inaugural.
> **Moses' face as he delivered the tablets was so bright**
> **that day...that the people of Israel could no more**
> **look right at him than stare into the sun.**
> How much more dazzling, then,
> the Government of Living Spirit...
> Bright as that government was, it would look
> downright dull alongside this new one...

121

> how much more this brightly shining government
> installed for eternity?"
> *2 CORINTHIANS 3:7-11 THE MESSAGE*

Here the scripture is speaking of the brilliant glory that radiated from Moses face after meeting with the Lord. It goes on to say, how we as His righteous ones have the same privilege as we encounter His presence.

> "But we all, with open face beholding as in a
> glass the glory of the Lord, are changed into
> the same image from glory to glory,
> even as by the Spirit of the Lord."
> *2 CORINTHIANS 3:18 KJ*

The Message Bible states it like this:

> "And when God is personally present, a living
> Spirit, that old, constricting legislation is recognized
> as obsolete. We're free of it! All of us!
> **Nothing between us and God,**
> **our faces shining with the brightness of His face.**
> **And so we are transfigured much like the Messiah,**
> **our lives gradually becoming**
> **brighter and more beautiful**
> **as God enters our lives and we become like Him."**
> *2 CORINTHIANS 3:18 THE MESSAGE*

Brighter and More Beautiful

In Ezekiel 28:12, Lucifer was described as, **"perfect (kalil) in beauty"** before he fell. Why? His perfect obedience as the high ranking arc angel made him blameless and holy as He walked among the stones of fire on the Holy Mount.

The word, "**perfect**" **is** "**kalil,**" #3632 translates as something **dedicated and altogether given to God.** When referring to a sacrifice, **it can mean a fiery sacrifice, constantly consumed—consumed in sacrificial fire as a holocaust. It is a whole burnt offering which has been fully and utterly committed to the flames.**

In our desire to raise prophetic kids we must inspire them to become altogether given to God and be consumed by His fiery love—so it's Him and Him alone that lives. Their agendas and self-will must be consumed as a sacrificial offering. They must know the **true meaning of beauty is really obedience and every time they obey, they become more beautiful.**

The enemy has gone forth in a wrath to "pimp" our kids with his worldly, disfigured image. He wants to smear their faces with his twisted lies and haughty, rebellious pride of what he calls beautiful. He brilliantly schemes to thieve their glory as his is stripped and lost forever! He lurks jealously as our emerging prophetic kids "re-present" Christ in the earth.

The prophet Moses bore this same spirit of prophecy in his body. Yes, he had made prophetic decrees that bound Pharaoh, the great dragon in the River Nile, but now his body transformed when he talked with God face to face.

"When Moses came down from Mount Sinai with the two tables of the Testimony in his hand,

**he did not know that the skin of his face shone and
sent forth beams
by reason of his speaking with the Lord."**
EXODUS 34:29 AMPLIFIED

"And all of us, as with unveiled face, [because we]
continued to behold {in the Word of God} as in
a mirror the glory of the Lord, are constantly being
transfigured into His very own image in ever
increasing splendor and from one degree of glory to
another, [for this comes] from the Lord..."
2 CORINTHIANS 3:18 AMPLIFIED

"**Transfigured**" translated in Greek is,
"metamorphoo," #3339 meaning a miracle of
transformation from an earthly form into a
supernatural form of radiance of garments and
glowing countenance.

This same word, "**metamorphoo**" is used in
Romans 12:2 when speaking of being transformed
by the renewing of our mind. It's saying we can be
"**transfigured**" as we match our thoughts to His.

This same word, "**metamorphoo**" is used on the
Mount of Transfiguration when Jesus revealed
Himself in His glorified body to Peter, James and
John six days after He said they would soon see His
kingdom coming in power.

**"And His appearance underwent a change...
His face shone clear and bright like the sun...
His clothing became as white as light."**
MATTHEW 17:2 & MARK 9:2 AMPLIFIED

Was Jesus giving them a flash forward of what
the power of His Kingdom looks like? Is it this

spirit of prophecy that unlocks the hidden Man of Jesus in us?   Isn't it His testimony in our prophetic kids that will bring glory to the Father?

> "To whom God would make known what is
> the riches of the glory of this mystery
> among the Gentiles; which is
> **Christ in you, the hope of glory."**
> *COLOSSIANS 1:27 KJ*

The Apostle Paul knew of this mystery. After his conversion, he retreated to the Arabian Desert for many years where he sought this God of indwelling glory.

> "God, who set me apart from my mother's womb
> and called me by his grace,
> **was pleased to reveal His Son in me... "**
> GALATIANS 1:15,16 NIV

This word **"reveal"** is the same word **"apokalupsis"** meaning to take the cover off or unveil.

How was this **"revealing"** actualized in Paul's ministry?   When Paul and Barnabus were at Lystra, they so testified and gave evidence of His glory and so accurately witnessed Jesus' person that the priest of Zeus brought bulls and garlands to offer in sacrifice to these mistaken gods.

> "The gods have come down to us in human form!"
> *ACTS 13:11 AMPLIFIED*

Stephen also tasted of this glory at a great price. When he was brought before the Sanhedrin, he preached about the God of glory appearing to

Abraham. The religious council actually stoned Stephen to death for carrying this same glory in his own body.

"Then all who sat in the council (Sanhedrin),
as they gazed intently at Stephen, saw that **his
face had the appearance of the face of an angel.**"
ACTS 6:15 AMPLIFIED

"But he, being full of the Holy Ghost,
looked up steadfastly into heaven,
and saw the glory of God, and Jesus
standing on the right hand of God. And said,
Behold, I see the heavens opened
and the Son of man
standing on the right hand of God."
ACTS 7:55,56 KJ

Celestial Charioteer

We might be thinking, Jeri, isn't this a bit edgy? Well, we can't forget about Elisha's glory being so indelible that it lingered in his bones even after his death. **When a dead man was tossed into his tomb, he revived and stood on his feet just by touching Elisha's bones. That's the tangible, indwelling glory, my friend. Let's catch the mantle!**

"Once while some Israelites were burying a man,
suddenly they saw a band of raiders;
so they threw the man's body into Elisha's tomb.
**When the body touched Elisha's bones,
the man came to life and stood up on his feet.**"
2 KINGS 13:21 NIV

Where did Elisha get this anointing—how did he catch Elijah's double portion mantle—the apostolic/prophetic anointing?   When Elisha realized his master, Elijah, was about to be taken away, he asked for a double portion of his spirit be upon him.

"… And Elisha said, I pray you, let a double portion
of your spirit be upon me.
He (Elijah) said, you have asked a hard thing.
**However, if you <u>see (ra'ah)</u> me when I am taken
from you, it shall be so for you—
but if not, it shall not be so."**
2 KINGS 2:9,10 AMPLIFIED

The word, "see" is the Hebrew word, "ra'ah," #7200.   One of the meanings is **to see things not perceived by the natural eyes—to see into the supernatural dimension.**

Our kids like Elisha must have these, "eyes wide open" so they can catch the double portion mantle of the prophetic/apostolic anointing.   Their vision and God's vision fusing into one—one sight—one perspective from God's point of view.

"… there appeared a chariot of fire,
and horses of fire, parted them both asunder;
and Elijah went up by a whirlwind into heaven.

And Elisha <u>saw, (ra'ah)</u> it and he cried,
**my father, my father, the chariot of Israel
and the <u>horsemen (parash)</u> thereof."**
2 KINGS 2;11,12 KJ

The word "horsemen," # 6571 is the Greek word, "parash" which translates a horse rider or more specifically, **a charioteer—the driver of a chariot.**

This time the Lord appeared to Elisha as the Heavenly Charioteer—the Celestial Driver of the Chariot. Often chariots had two drivers. **Elijah was about to have the ultimate limousine service!— transportation by The Lord of glory Himself! What a sight as the two rode side by side—cracking the skyways in glory.** And yes, Elisha saw, "ra'ah" it all!

Elisha had to peer within the glory cloud that had overshadowed Elijah's ministry. His eyes had to "see," "ra'ah," the Charioteer, Jesus, if he were to catch the same mantle. Something was happening—his eyes were catching a glimpse of God's government within the cloud.

Like Ezekiel, he was seeing the chariot of cherubim, dart like lightning flashes. Over their heads was dazzling crystal stretched across the firmament and above a sapphire throne—the life and holy authority of Jesus. Elisha learned by heart about God's Kingdom authority—veiled within the glory cloud was Jesus enthroned in all power and dominion—every enemy subdued!

God needs our vision coupled with His to perform the impossible. God needs our prophetic sight fused with His—the two must move in tandem—an optical fusion that releases that which is in heaven to earth.

This supernatural vision is crucial to our prophetic kids just as it was in Elisha's ministry. When he and his fearful servant were besieged, Elisha prayer that God would open his servant's eyes and let him **"see," (ra'ah)** into the Spirit realm. It was only then that he could **"see"** the wonder of a whole mountainside full of horses and chariots of fire surrounding Elisha!—much more than the enemy had.

Elisha had learned well—learned by heart—the supernatural reality of the glory cloud overshadowing him—infused with Kingdom authority and dominion. **The Heavenly Charioteer—Jesus the Celestial Rider was surely with him just as he had been with Elijah.**

Resurrection Power
---◯◯---

In closing, as an inspiration for us all, I want to share a scientific truth that holds amazing Spiritual insight. It concerns the famous formula that the renowned physicist Albert Einstein discovered, $E = MC$ squared. This mathematical formula proved that the substance or mass of anything multiplied times the speed of light squared would equal the energy contained in that substance. In other words, he discovered that all matter or molecular weight is made up of energy that can be harnessed and released.

Using his formula, nuclear physicists have recently proven that if the mass of one ordinary, normal-sized tree could be converted into energy—that one tree would meet all the energy needs of the USA for 10 years. What a power house inside that simple tree—but how much more power in us as the sons of God.

Oh Lord, help us raise prophetic kids that convert all their being and their very substance into the same power—the same energy that raised Christ from the dead.

"I pray also that the eyes of your heart may be enlightened in order that you may know
the hope to which he has called you,
the riches of his glorious inheritance in the saints,
and his incomparable great power for us who believe. **That power is like the working of his mighty strength, which he exerted in Christ when he raised him from the dead** and seated him at his right hand in the heavenly realms, far above all rule and authority, power and dominion, and every title that can be given, not only in the present age but also in the one to come. And God placed all things under his feet and appointed him to be head over everything for the church, which is his body, the fullness of him who fills everything in every way."
EPHESIANS 1:18-23 NIV

May the Spirit of this book exhilarate your holy imagination—stoke the fire and fan the flame that burns within. All my love to you, my friends, as we continue on our journey as sons and daughters of the Most High God.

Additional copies of this book and Jeri's new release,
"The Perfect Heart" available at:
www.gracegrace.com.
Distributed by www.anchordistributors.com.

Check out other "Resources for Prophetic Kids" at www.gracegrace.com.

Coming Soon...Prophetic CD's...DVD's...Journals...more prophetic
books & resources for children's ministries and anointed family times.

Encounter heaven in your home ...soak with worship artist Grace Williams
Listen and purchase her complete line of CD's at our web site.

Contact Information:

Mashach Publishing
www.gracegrace.com
949-813-3124
jeri@gracegrace.com
1001 Avenida Pico, Suite C #331
San Clemente, CA 92673